Edith C Kenyon

Scenes in the Life of the Royal Family

Edith C Kenyon

Scenes in the Life of the Royal Family

ISBN/EAN: 9783742819772

Manufactured in Europe, USA, Canada, Australia, Japa

Cover: Foto ©ninafisch / pixelio.de

Manufactured and distributed by brebook publishing software (www.brebook.com)

Edith C Kenyon

Scenes in the Life of the Royal Family

BY SPECIAL PERMISSION OF HER MAJESTY THE QUEEN.

SCENES IN THE LIFE OF
THE ROYAL FAMILY.

By EDITH C. KENYON.

LONDON:
W. NICHOLSON AND SONS,
20, WARWICK SQUARE, PATERNOSTER ROW, E.C.,
AND ALBION WORKS, WAKEFIELD.

BY SPECIAL PERMISSION OF HER MAJESTY THE QUEEN.

SCENES IN THE LIFE OF

THE ROYAL FAMILY.

By EDITH C. KENYON,

AUTHOR OF "SCENES IN THE LIFE OF THE PRINCESS ALICE," "JACK'S COUSIN KATE," "THE HEROINE OF BROOKLEIGH," &C. &C.

LONDON:
W. NICHOLSON AND SONS,
20, WARWICK SQUARE, PATERNOSTER ROW, E.C.,
AND ALBION WORKS, WAKEFIELD.

UPB

PREFACE.

IT is with gratitude that I acknowledge the great kindness of Her Majesty in granting me permission to publish, also, this little volume about the Royal Family in this year of her Jubilee.

The readers of "SCENES IN THE LIFE OF THE PRINCESS ALICE," will, I trust, receive with pleasure this additional, and, in a measure, supplementary volume to the above. For while one book treats almost exclusively of the late Princess Alice of England, the other is about her parents, brothers and sisters, whose lives were so intimately interwoven with her own, and who were so inexpressibly dear to herself.

EDITH C. KENYON.

March, 1887.

CONTENTS.

Page.

CHAP. I.—QUEEN VICTORIA'S INFANCY. Birth—Christening—A Narrow Escape—The Duke of Kent Playing with his Baby—After his Death mistaking her Uncle for him 11

CHAP. II.—QUEEN VICTORIA'S CHILDHOOD. Riding and Walking—Scene in Kensington Gardens—On the Sands at Ramsgate—Learning to Read—Impatience in Learning Music—Truthfulness—The Young Harpist and the Princess—At Breakfast in the Open Air, &c. 19

CHAP. III.—MORE SCENES FROM QUEEN VICTORIA'S CHILDHOOD. The Young Princess Visiting the Tomb of "The Dairyman's Daughter" with her Mother—In the Jeweller's Shop—Falling down in a Garden—Witty Remarks about Cornelians—The Princess in Church —The Princess Watering her Flowers—At a Bazaar—A little Self-willed—The Confirmation of the Princess—Her Love of Music ... 27

CHAP. IV.—IMPORTANT AND SUGGESTIVE EVENTS. The Princess learns the Secret of her Heritage—First State Appearance at Queen Adelaide's Drawing-room—Prince Albert as a Baby—The first Meeting of Princess Victoria and Prince Albert 39

CHAP. V.—THE ACCESSION. Queen Victoria—Her Majesty's First Privy Council—Proclamation of the Queen—Her Majesty Emotion—Her Desire to be Alone for a Short Time 51

CONTENTS.

	Page.
CHAP. VI.—THE YOUNG QUEEN. Leaving Kensington for Buckingham Palace—Going to Dissolve Parliament—The Duke of Wellington bringing the First Death Warrant for Her Majesty to Sign—The Queen's Reverence for the Lord's Day—Reproving her Lady for Unpunctuality—Letter from Prince Albert	64
CHAP. VII.—THE CORONATION. Preliminary Arrangements—Crowding of Ladies and Gentlemen to the Abbey in the Early Morning—The Royal Procession—The Coronation—Lord Rolle's Disaster—Return from the Abbey—Little Dash	73
CHAP. VIII.—THE QUEEN'S ENGAGEMENT TO PRINCE ALBERT. Difficulties of the Queen's Position—Visit of the Two Princes—The Queen's Proposal—Letters on the Subject—Her Majesty's Declaration to Her Privy Council	93
CHAP. IX.—MARRIAGE OF QUEEN VICTORIA AND PRINCE ALBERT. Prince Albert being Invested with the Garter—Sorrowful Leave-taking with the Prince's Grandmother—A Parting Scene—Eôs, the Beautiful Greyhound—Arrival at Buckingham Palace—The Royal Wedding ...	106
CHAP. X.—EARLY MARRIED LIFE. Prince Albert's parting with his Father—Writing to his Grandmother—Easter Communion with the Queen—A Serious Accident—Parting with Prince Ernest—Sketch of the Daily Life of the Prince and Queen—Their interest in Art—Mendelssohn's Reminiscences	123
CHAP. XI.—THE YOUNG ROYAL PARENTS. More about Prince Albert—His and the Queen's love of the Country—Birth of the Princess Royal—Birth of the Prince of Wales—Christmas-trees—The Titles of the Infant Prince	138
CHAP. XII.—THE QUEEN'S FIRST VISIT TO SCOTLAND. Reception at Edinburgh—Anecdotes—Quotations from the Queen's Book—Letters to her Majesty's Scottish Subjects	147
CHAP. XIII—MORE ABOUT THE ROYAL CHILDREN. The Little Princess Royal—The Little Prince of Wales—Lady Bloomfield's Reminiscences—The Princess Royal Travelling in Scotland with her Parents—Staying at Blair Athole—Anecdote of the Queen—Other Incidents of Life in the Highlands	158
CHAP. XIV.—VERY DIFFERENT SCENES. Visit from the King Louis Philippe of France—His Reception—Driving out with the Queen—Investiture with the Garter	171

CONTENTS.

CHAP. XV.—OSBORNE. Sir Charles Lyell's Notes of a Visit there—The Children's Workplace and Play Ground 176

CHAP. XVI.—BALMORAL. Extracts from First Letters of the Prince and Queen from Balmoral—Deer-Stalking—Reading and Quoting Poetry —Account of the Scotch Home in Greville's Journal—Her Majesty's Visit to Poor Old Women 182

CHAP. XVII.—THE FIRST WEDDING IN OUR ROYAL FAMILY. Prince Frederick William of Prussia's Proposal to the Princess Royal—Their Engagement—Confirmation of the Princess—Her Serious Accident— The Queen's Speech to the Officers and Soldiers from the Crimea— The Wedding—The Departure of the Princess for her New Home ... 193

CHAP. XVIII.—GLAD SCENES AND SORROWFUL. The Prince Consort and Queen on their way to Visit the Princess Royal—Death of "Carl" a Trusted Valet—The Joyful Meeting—Glimpses of Princess Beatrice and of Princess Alice—Death of the Duchess of Kent ... 203

CHAP. XIX.—THE DEATH OF THE PRINCE CONSORT. The Prince Consort's Letter to the Duchess of Kent on the Anniversary of his Wedding Day—Last Events of his Life—His Illness—Death—Funeral —Words of the Poet Laureate 211

CHAP. XX.—MARRIAGES IN THE ROYAL FAMILY. The Queen's Sympathy with the Sufferers from the Hartley Colliery Accident—Dr. Macleod—Marriage of Princess Alice and Prince Louis of Hesse— Presentation of a Bible from the Widows of England to the Queen —The Prince of Wales's Marriage—The Princess of Wales... ... 223

CHAP. XXI.—LATER SCENES. The Marquis of Lorne—His Marriage with the Princess Louise—Story of the Marchioness of Lorne—Serious Illness of the Prince of Wales—The Thanksgiving Day—Death of Dr. Macleod—Attempts on the Queen's Life—Her Majesty's Bravery —Princess Beatrice—The Duke of Albany's Marriage and Death— The Queen Opening the Indian and Colonial Exhibition 233

SCENES IN THE LIFE OF
THE ROYAL FAMILY.

CHAPTER I.

QUEEN VICTORIA'S INFANCY.

BIRTH—CHRISTENING—A NARROW ESCAPE—THE DUKE OF KENT PLAYING WITH HIS BABY—AFTER HIS DEATH—MISTAKING HER UNCLE FOR HIM.

IN this year of our Queen's Jubilee, it is both pleasant and profitable to glance at some of the most striking scenes in Her Majesty's own life and in the lives of those to whom she has indeed been a most inestimable wife and mother.

In the year 1819, when many limping Subalterns or scarred veterans from the battle-ground of Waterloo, still continued to be heroes of distant towns and villages, or lions at such places as Bath or Tunbridge, a little child was born in the Duchess of Kent's rooms at Kensington Palace, on the 24th of May, who has long been dear to the hearts of all loyal English men and women.

There were ostensibly several lives between that of the infant and the throne, and yet with rare prophetic foresight, her father, the Duke of Kent, who was not destined while on earth to see the fruition of his hopes, would show his baby to his friends, saying proudly,—

"Look at her well, for she will yet be Queen of England."

The baby's Grandfather still lived, and his three older sons; her parents might yet have a son, but, still, with that rare intuition with which sometimes thoughtful men surprise one, the tall and stately father pointed out his infant as the heiress to the crown.

At the baby's christening, the gold font was brought down from the tower, and the Archbishop of Canterbury assisted by the Bishop of London baptised the child, giving to her the names of Alexandrina Victoria. The former was after the Emperor Alexander of Russia, who was one of the baby's godfathers, the latter after her mother.

It is said there was a proposal to name the little Princess, Georgiana, after her grandfather, George III., and the Prince Regent, who was present, and who was the other godfather. But to this the latter objected, as he would not permit his name to stand second on the list. It is also stated that her father, the Duke of Kent, wished to name his child Elizabeth, that name being popular with English people, but the Prince Regent only gave at the Baptism the name of Alexandrina. Upon which the Duke asked for another name to be added.

The Prince replied,—

"Give her her mother's name also then; but it cannot precede that of the Emperor."

The baby's godmothers were the Queen Dowager of Wurtemburg (the Princess Royal), represented by Princess Augusta, and the Duchess Dowager of Coburg, mother of the Duchess of Kent, and grandmother of both our Queen and the Prince Consort, represented by the Duchess of Gloucester (Princess Mary).

Prince Leopold, the uncle of our Queen, who was to her as a second father, and one of her kindest and wisest friends, was a guest at the christening. He who had been so happy two years before, was then a widower and childless. It had been hard for him to be present, but he felt it to be his duty and he made the effort.

In the life of the Prince Consort, we are told that it was not until a great misfortune happened to her, that he had the courage to look upon the blooming face of his infant niece. With great and manly pity and wise tenderness he overcame this reluctance, as we shall see.

When the baby Princess was little more than six months old, her parents having gone with her to Woolbrook Cottage, Sidmouth in Devonshire, she almost lost her life by what might have been a serious accident.

A boy shooting sparrows, fired so near to the house, that his shot shattered one of the nursery windows and passed close to the head of the child as it was in her nurse's arms. We can imagine the scene, the terror of the nurse, the distress of the Duchess, and the anger and apprehension of the Duke, to say nothing of the horror and unhappiness of the unfortunate offender, who had thus nearly shot the precious infant.

Not many days after that there was great trouble at Woolbrook Cottage. The Duke had been taking a long walk with his equerry and good friend, Captain Conray, and he came in tired, and with his feet so wet that it was suggested he should change his boots. But the proud and happy father saw his little one before he had done so, and the baby, little knowing what she did, stretched out her arms and laughed at him, and so he lingered playing with her instead. And, consequently, he took the cold which finally settled on his lungs and proved so fatal.

The Duchess of Kent had been married before, when

she was only seventeen, to Prince Emich Charles of Leiningen, and she had one daughter by that marriage, the Princess Feodore, who was nine or ten years old at the time of her stepfather's illness. Long afterwards, she wrote to Her Majesty, that she well remembered that dreadful time at Sidmouth, and how she prayed on her knees "that God would not let your dear father die. I loved him dearly," she said, "he was always so kind to me."

The Duke died after having been just able to sign the will, which left the Duchess guardian to his little girl, and appointed General Wetherell and Captain Conray trustees of his estate, for the benefit of his widow and daughter. He was buried at Windsor by torchlight, on the night of the 12th of February, 1820. For long, the tolling of the bell from out of the dark tower of Windsor, which proclaimed that a Royal Duke had passed away, would be remembered.

But the stately dark funeral procession, veiled by the shades of night, and typical, indeed, of the Valley of the Shadow of Death, was but the outward manifestation of the desolation which reigned in the Sidmouth Cottage. The young Duchess, only a little over thirty, found herself left in a foreign land, of which, it is said, she scarcely understood the language, deprived of a kind husband, and the guardian of a little child who was destined, so her husband believed (and as events proved rightly), to wear a crown. She was not rich, but she had what would have been affluence in her own country, her mother and her friends were there, but in England her expenses were great in proportion to her income, here, she might be misunderstood, interfered with, censured. Surely the thought must have come to her, that she would take her child, her children, and, disregarding or doubting her husband's strong feeling, as to who would be the future Queen of England, retire to the country of her youth.

Let us look at her as she sits there, pondering over matters in her grief. We are told she had a fine figure, good features, brown hair and eyes, a pretty pink colour, winning manners, and that she was a handsome, charming and attractive woman. She was accomplished, too, particularly as regards music, and she was graceful. But there was something better behind all this, and that was she possessed sound common sense, unflinching self-sacrifice, and a power of steady adherence to what she perceived to be her duty, which proved to be of incalculable service to our Queen and to our country. For the widowed Duchess resolved to stay in England.

She was not left quite desolate, however, for Prince Leopold hastened to her with his kind and generous support and sympathy. And, two days afterwards, he accompanied her and her baby to London. The story

HER MOST GRACIOUS MAJESTY QUEEN VICTORIA.

runs that the infant, being held up to the carriage window to bid the assembled population of Sidmouth farewell, sported, laughed and patted the glass with her pretty dimpled hands, in happy unconsciousness of her heavy loss. The little one mistook the Duke of York for her father, when he came on a visit of condolence, and also, afterwards, and by stretching out her hands to him in that belief, won from him the promise, as he clasped her in his arms, that he would be her father.

The happy baby formed a striking contrast to her unhappy mother, as she generally received the addresses of condolence with her infant in her arms.

Interesting stories are told of the baby, at fifteen months old, riding out in her little carriage, accompanied by her half sister, Princess Feodore. The child liked to be noticed, and would say "Lady" and "good morning," and would hold out her soft dimpled hand to be kissed. Her large blue eyes, beautiful bloom, and fair complexion, made her a model of infantine beauty.

A private soldier, Maloney by name, on one occasion claimed the honour of saving the life of our future Queen. He was in Kensington garden, when the child in her pony-carriage came up. A page was leading the pony, a lady walked on one side, and a young woman beside the carriage. But a great water-dog, suddenly running up, got between the pony's legs, causing it to plunge on one side and overturn the carriage. The little one was thrown out, head foremost, but Maloney caught her by her dress and swung her into his arms. He restored her to the lady, and was much praised by the bystanders for his rescue of the Princess.

CHAPTER II.

QUEEN VICTORIA'S CHILDHOOD.

RIDING AND WALKING—SCENE IN KENSINGTON GARDENS—ON THE SANDS AT RAMSGATE—LEARNING TO READ—IMPATIENCE IN LEARNING MUSIC—TRUTHFULNESS—THE YOUNG HARPIST AND THE PRINCESS—AT BREAKFAST IN THE OPEN AIR, ETC.

WE are told that very simple was the life which the Duchess of Kent lived with her two children at Kensington. At eight in summer the family party met at breakfast, after breakfast the two Princesses would walk or drive for an hour. An old pensioner was often the attendant of the Princess during her donkey-rides in the Park. The little girl was sometimes self-willed and would not walk when the ladies who accompanied her thought she should, and, then, the old soldier would try to persuade her.

"Will my Princess walk?" he would ask.

But there would only be for answer a determined little shake of the head.

"It will do my Princess so much good to walk a little—only a little."

But another shake of the little head would once more baffle the old man.

"Will my Princess let me lift her down to run on the nice soft grass?" would then perhaps win the child's ready compliance.

A writer in a contemporary newspaper thus describes how he saw the Royal infant one day in Kensington Gardens, "A party consisting of several ladies, a young child, and two men-servants, having in charge a donkey, gaily caparisoned with blue ribbons, and accoutred for the use of the infant." Having said how he found the Duchess of Kent and her daughter formed the centre of the group, he went on, "On approaching the Royal party, the infant Princess, observing my respectful recognition, nodded and wished me a good morning with much liveliness, as she skipped along between her mother and her sister, Princess Feodore, holding a hand of each." She was taught carefully to return all the salutations that were made to her as she passed on, "Her Royal Highness," continued the writer, "is remarkably beautiful, and her gay and animated countenance bespeaks perfect health and good temper. Her complexion is excessively fair, and her cheeks blooming. She bears a striking resemblance to her late Royal father, and indeed to every member of our reigning family."

Again, a writer in Fraser's Magazine tells us how he

saw the Princess, when five years old playing on the Ramsgate sands, in her simple dress,—"A plain straw bonnet with a white ribbon round the crown, a coloured muslin frock, looking gay and cheerful, and as pretty a pair of shoes on as pretty a pair of feet as I ever remember to have seen."

"Near her was her mother, standing talking to William Wilberforce and laughing when an unexpected wave would suddenly ripple over the feet of the Princess." We are told that the writer watched the Duchess and her daughter proceed up the High Street to their residence, and saw the child run back to put some silver in the lap of an old Irish woman sitting on a door step.

From ten to twelve Princess Victoria would receive instruction, often from her mother. The lady is reported to have said, "I am anxious to bring you up as a good woman, and then you will be a good Queen also."

But we are also told the child was kept in ignorance of what was likely to be her future. Her grandmother writing to her mother recommended the Duchess "not to tease her with learning while she was so young."

We are told, however, that she mastered the alphabet almost before she could express her thoughts in words. She grew impatient when she was learning her letters and demanded,*

---

* This striking little incident is from "Our Queen."

"What good this? What good that?"

"Mamma can know all that is in the great books on the table, because she knows her letters, but her little daughter cannot," was the reply.

"I learn, too, I learn very quick," responded the child.

When she began to learn the piano, too, the same impatient spirit showed itself, but also the same reasonableness upon conviction. The Princess was told that she must make herself mistress of the piano.

It was a new thought. "I am to be mistress of my piano, am I?" asked she.

"Yes, indeed, Princess."

"Then what would you think of me if I became mistress at once?"

That she was told was impossible. There was no Royal road to music. Experience and much practice were essential.

"Oh, there is no Royal road to music, eh? No Royal road, and I am not mistress of my pianoforte? But I will be, I assure you; and the Royal road is this."—Whereupon she closed the piano, locked it, and put the key into her pocket, saying, "There! That is being mistress of the piano! And the Royal road to learning is never to take a lesson till you are in the humour to do it."

However, when the joke was over, she volunteered herself to go on with the lesson.

Miss Tytler tells us a better story, which she says the late Bishop Wilberforce was told by Dr. Davys, who taught the young Princess at one time. He said,

"The Queen always had, from my first knowing her, a most striking regard to truth. I remember when I had been teaching her one day, she was very impatient for the lesson to be over, once or twice rather refractory. The Duchess of Kent came in and asked how she had behaved. Lehzen (Baroness Lehzen was one of the Queen's earliest guardians) said,

"Oh, once she was rather troublesome."

The Princess touched her and said, "No, Lehzen, twice, don't you remember?" The Duchess of Kent, too, was a woman of great truth.

After lessons the Princess would play, but even during playhours, she was taught to attend to what she was doing, and finish what she began.

One day, whilst amusing herself in making a small haycock, some other mimic occupation caught her childish fancy, and down the small rake was thrown, while she rushed off to the fresh attraction. But that was not to be allowed.

"No, no, Princess, you must always complete what you have commenced," said her governess. And the little haycock had to be completed.

The child longed sometimes for companions of her own age, Princess Feodore being so much older than herself. At one time her mother, doubtless knowing that, and knowing, too, what great delight the Princess took in music, sent for a child-performer on the harp, who was much noted at the time, and who was called Lyra, to play for her. On one occasion, when the Princess seemed thoroughly absorbed with one of her favourite airs which Lyra was playing, the Duchess left the room for a few moments. When she returned, the music had ceased, and the Princess had beguiled the young musician from her instrument to look at her costly toys.

The children were found sitting side by side on the hearthrug, surrounded by the Princess's playthings from which she was selecting not a few for poor little Lyra's acceptance.

We have a glimpse of the Princess given us by Charles Knight, as he saw her in 1827, in his "Passages of a Working Life."

"I delighted to walk in Kensington Gardens," he observes. "As I passed along the broad central walk, I saw a group on the lawn before the Palace, which to my mind was a vision of exquisite loveliness. The Duchess of Kent and her daughter, whose years then numbered nine, are breakfasting in the open air—a single page attending upon them at a respectful distance; the matron looking on with eyes of love, whilst the soft English face is bright with smiles. What a beautiful characteristic it seemed to me of the training of this Royal girl that she should not have been taught to shrink from the public eye; that she should not have been burdened with a premature conception of her probable high destiny; that she should enjoy the freedom and simplicity of a child's nature; that she should not be restrained when she starts up from the breakfast-table and runs to gather a flower in the adjoining parterre; that her merry laugh should be as fearless as the notes of the thrush in the groves round her. I passed on, and blessed her; and I thank God that I have lived to see the golden fruits of such training."*

We are told that the Princess asked one day, when she was returning from a drive in the Park why the gentlemen took their hats off to her and not to her sister, the Princess Feodore, but we are not told what answer was made to the puzzling question. When Sir Walter Scott was presented to the fair-haired child in 1828, he fancied some bird of the air must have conveyed the important secret to her of the likelihood of her becoming the Queen, but we are told on good authority that he was wrong. The secret was not revealed to her for some years.

When Princess Victoria was only five years old she

---

* From "Queen Victoria," published by Messrs. Partridge.

was at Claremont, Miss Tytler says, "making music and motion in the quiet house with her gleeful laughter and pattering feet, so happy in being with her uncle that she could look back on this visit as the brightest of her early holidays. 'This place,' the Queen wrote to the King of the Belgians long afterwards, 'has a peculiar charm for us both, and to me it brings back recollections of the happiest days of my otherwise dull childhood,—when I experienced such kindness from you, dearest Uncle, kindness which has ever since continued. ....Victoria plays with my old bricks, and I see her running and jumping in the flower-garden, as *old*, though I still feel *little* Victoria of former days used to do.'"

CHAPTER III.

MORE SCENES FROM QUEEN VICTORIA'S CHILDHOOD.

THE YOUNG PRINCESS VISITING THE TOMB OF THE DAIRYMAN'S DAUGHTER WITH HER MOTHER — IN THE JEWELLER'S SHOP — FALLING DOWN IN A GARDEN—WITTY REMARK ABOUT CORNELIANS—THE PRINCESS IN CHURCH —THE PRINCESS WATERING HER FLOWERS — AT A BAZAAR — A LITTLE SELF-WILLED — THE CONFIRMATION OF THE PRINCESS — HER LOVE OF MUSIC.

IN the summer of 1831, we are told, the Duchess of Kent and her daughter spent three pleasant months at Norris Castle in the Isle of Wight, and the Princess became much attached to the fair island which was so intimately connected with the joys of later years.

Miss Greenwood tells us of a tourist who happened to visit Arreton Churchyard at the time of which we are speaking, and who, on approaching the tomb of the "Dairyman's daughter," found a lady and a young girl sitting beside the mound.

"The girl was reading aloud in a full melodious voice the touching tale of the Christian maiden. He found, afterwards, on speaking to the sexton, that the two ladies were the Duchess of Kent and Princess Victoria.

We turn from that beautiful and characteristic incident to look with pleasure on another very different scene which illustrates the results of such teaching as the future Queen received.

The Princess, we are told, was in the habit of amusing herself by going *incognito* in a carriage to different shops, not only to purchase articles for herself, but to watch with interest what others were doing and purchasing. One day, at a jeweller's shop, she perceived a young and intelligent lady, who was busily looking over some gold chains for the neck.

Having fixed upon the one she would like she enquired the price, but upon finding it was more than she expected, she regarded the chain very wistfully and asked,—

"Could it not be offered cheaper?"

"Impossible," was the reply.

The would-be purchaser was obliged reluctantly to lay the chain aside and content herself with a cheaper article.

After she had left the shop, Princess Victoria, who had been much interested in what she had seen, inquired of the jeweller whom the young lady was, and on receiving satisfactory information, she ordered the much admired chain to be packed up and sent to her.

A card was forwarded with it which intimated that,

"Princess Victoria was so well pleased in observing that the young lady, who had been so much taken up with the beauty and workmanship of the chain had yet so much command of her passions as not to suffer those to overcome her prudence, that she desired her to accept the chain which she so much admired, in the hope that she would always persevere in that laudable line of conduct upon which female happiness so much depended."

A Yorkshire lady has given us an amusing glimpse of the young Princess under very different circumstances.

She went with her mother, the Duchess of Kent, on a visit to Earl Fitzwilliam, at Wentworth House, and, while there, found great delight in running about alone in the gardens and shrubberies. She was amusing herself thus one wet morning, when an old gardener, who was not aware of the little visitor's name and rank, saw her about to descend a treacherous piece of ground from the terrace, and called out, "Be careful, Miss, its slape!" meaning "its slippery." The Princess, thus admonished, turned round with the enquiry,

"What's slape?"

But immediately afterwards she received a practical answer, for her feet flew from under her, and she fell down.

As the old gardener assisted her to rise, he replied, "That's slape, Miss."

Another account says that it was Earl Fitzwilliam himself who called out,—

"Now your Royal Highness has an explanation of the term "slape" both theoretically and practically."

"Yes, my Lord," she replied, "I think I have. I shall never forget the word 'slape.'"

Another time, we are told, the Princess showed that she was possessed of very ready wit. Her teacher had been reading to her in her classical history the story of "Cornelia, the mother of the Gracchi — how she had proudly presented her sons to the first of the Roman ladies with the words,—

"These are my jewels."

"She should have said my Cornelians," immediately replied the Princess.

Leigh Hunt gives us a pleasing glimpse of Her Royal Highness in the "*Old Court Suburb.*"

"We remember well," he says, "the peculiar pleasure which it gave us to see the future Queen, the first time we ever did see her, coming up a cross path from the Bayswater gate, with a girl of her own age by her side, whose hand she was holding as if she loved her. A magnificent footman in scarlet came behind her, with the splendidest pair of calves in white stockings which we ever beheld. He looked somehow like a gigantic fairy, personating, for his little lady's sake, the grandest kind of footman he could think of; and his calves he seemed to have made out of a couple of the biggest chain. lamps in the possession of the godmother of Cinderella."

In a cottage not far from Claremont, there dwelt the aged mother of Miss Jane Porter, the author of "The Scottish Chiefs," "Thaddeus of Warsaw," &c., with her and her sister. The authoress had many opportunities of observing Princess Victoria as a child, and in a private letter, written soon after her accession to the throne, she said,

"My mother had warmly loved the noble virtues of Princess Charlotte. She did not less admire their corresponding continuance in Prince Leopold; and she delighted in thinking the young Princess Victoria resembled Princess Charlotte in her infancy. My mother, attended by a favourite little white poodle dog, with a crook-headed stick in her hand, assisting, but not yet supporting her still unenfeebled steps, generally chose her places for walking where she would be most likely to meet the young hope of England taking her morning exercise; and great was the pleasure with which she marked every animated movement of the youthful Victoria, whether walking by the side of her governess, or running forward in the eagerness of childhood's happy impulses, with a bounding elasticity of active enjoyment which full health only, or the Spring of earliest youth can know.........In describing the infancy of the Princess, I would say she was a beautiful child, with a cherubic form of features, clustered round by glossy fair ringlets. Her complexion was remarkably transparent, with a soft but often heightening tinge of the sweet blushrose upon her cheeks, that imparted a peculiar brilliancy to her clear blue eyes. Whenever she met any strangers in her usual paths she always seemed by the quickness of her glance to inquire who and what they were? The intelligence of her countenance was extraordinary at her very early age, but might easily be accounted for on perceiving the extraordinary intelligence of her mind.

*"I remember a little incident that may illustrate this. One Sunday, at Esher Church, when the Princess Victoria, might be about six years old, my attention was particularly attracted to the Claremont pew, in which she and the Duchess of Kent and her Royal Uncle (then the widowed King Leopold) sat. It occupies a colonnaded recess, elevated a little, in the interior south wall of the Church. Parallel to it runs a small gallery of pews, from one of which (my mother's) being directly opposite to the Royal seat, I could see all that passed. I should not voluntarily have so employed myself at Church, but I had seen a wasp skim-

---

* These reminiscences are from Mr. G. B. Smith's "Life of Queen Victoria."

HAMPTON COURT, GARDEN FRONT.

THE CORONATION, WESTMINISTER ABBEY.

ming backwards and forwards, over the head and before the unveiled summer bonnet of the little Princess, and I could not forbear watching the dangerous insect, fearing it would sting her face. She, totally unobserving it, had meanwhile fixed her eyes on the clergyman, who had taken his seat in the pulpit to preach the sermon, and she never withdrew them thence for a moment during his whole discourse.

"Next day, a lady, personally intimate at Claremont, called at our humble little abode, and I remarked to her the scene I had witnessed the preceding morning at Church; wondering what could possibly have engaged the Princess's attention so unrecedingly to the face of the Rev. Dr. ——, a person totally unknown to her, and whose countenance, though expressive of good sense, was wiry and roughhewn, and could present nothing pleasing enough to fix the eyes of a child.

"'It was not himself that attracted her fixed eyes,' replied our visitor, 'it was the sermon he was preaching. For it is a custom with her illustrious instructress to inquire of Princess Victoria, not only the text of the discourse, but also the heads of its leading subjects. Hence she neither saw the wasp when in front of her, nor heard the whisking of the protective handkerchief behind her. Her whole mind was bound up in her task —a rare faculty of concentration in any individual, therefore more wonderful in one hardly beyond infancy. And with a most surprising understanding of the subjects, she never fails performing her task in a manner that might grace much older years."

Lord Albemarle in his autobiography tells us, "One of my occupations of a morning, while waiting for the Duke; was to watch from my windows the movements of a bright pretty little girl, seven years of age. She was in the habit of watering the plants immediately under the window. It was amusing to see how impartially she divided the contents of her watering-pot between the flowers and her own little feet. Her simple but becoming dress contrasted favourably with the gorgeous apparel now worn by the little damsels of the rising generation,—a large fichu round the neck was the only ornament she wore. The young lady I am describing was Princess Victoria."

We learn that the Princess was very carefully trained in prudence, economy and self-control in the matter of expenditure. We have seen how the Princess admired prudence and self-control in another, we shall now see how those qualities were not only theoretically but practically learned by herself. Miss Martineau tells us a story illustrative of this:—"It became known at Tunbridge Wells that the Princess had been unable to buy a box at the Bazaar, because she had spent her money. At this Bazaar she had bought presents for almost all her relations, and had laid out her last shilling, when she remembered one cousin more, and saw a box, price half-a-crown, which would suit him. The shop-people of course placed the box with the other purchases, but the little lady's governess admonished them by saying, 'No; you see the Princess has not got the money, of course, she cannot have the box.' This being perceived, the next offer was to lay by the box till it could be purchased, and the answer was, 'Oh, well, if you will be so good as to do that.'

"On quarter-day before seven in the morning, the Princess appeared on her donkey to claim her purchase."

The little Princess, though thus carefully trained, was not without a certain amount of wilfulness, but, as we have hinted before, when she became convinced that another way was better than her own she was quite reasonable enough to take it.

*Once, she was playing with a dog of uncertain temper; and she was warned to desist. She was not afraid, however, and continued her frolic. Presently, we are told the dog made a snap at her hand.

"Oh, Princess, I am afraid you are bitten," said the person who had cautioned her, running to her assistance.

"Oh, thanks, thanks!" said Her Royal Highness,

* "Famous Girls," by J. M. Darton.

"You are right, and I am wrong: but he didn't bite me, he only warned me. I shall be careful in future."

The Princess Victoria was confirmed on the 30th of August 1835 by the Archbishop of Canterbury, assisted by the Bishop of London, in the Chapel Royal at St. James's.

Besides the Princess and the Duchess of Kent, only the King, Queen Adelaide and the Duchess of Saxe-Weimar, with some other members of the Royal Family were present.

"I witnessed," said one who was present, "a beautiful touching scene the day before yesterday at the Chapel Royal, St. James's—the confirmation of the Princess Victoria by the Archbishop of Canterbury. The Royal Family only were present. The ceremony was very affecting; the beautiful, pathetic and parental exhortation of the Archbishop on the duties she was called on to fulfil, the great responsibilities that her high station imposed on her, the struggles she must prepare for, between the allurements of the world and the dictates and claims of religion and justice, and the necessity of her looking up for counsel to her Maker in all the trying scenes that awaited her, was most impressive. She was led up by the King, and knelt before the altar. Her mother stood by her side, weeping audibly, as did indeed the Queen and the other ladies present. King William frequently shed tears, nodding his head at each impressive part of the discourse. The little Princess herself was drowned in tears.

"When the service was over, the King led the Princess up to the Queen to salute her, and then, the Royal Duchesses who were present."

The same interesting narative tells us that "the Princess, when a mere child, drew her Uncle to the window to observe the beauties of an autumnal sunset; and when hearing for the first time Beethoven's 'Hallelujah,' the celebrated passage, 'The exalted Son of God,' affected her so powerfully that for several minutes she sat spell-bound, unable to give expression to the admiration and delight she had experienced. The nation is indebted to the Bishop of Salisbury, the Archbishop of Canterbury, and the Bishop of Lincoln, for the sound and careful education of the Princess."

Besides sound religious training, Her Majesty had a thorough knowledge of the history of her own country, we are told, the laws by which it is governed as well as the literature and "science by which it is blessed." The names and works of poets were as familiar as "household words."

She was able, we are also told; to read Horace with ease, and in drawing, in other circumstances, she might "have made for herself an eminent position as an artist."

As for her singing, Thomas Moore tells us, in his Diary, that when only twelve years old, he heard her sing a duet with her mother, and several very pretty German songs by herself. One or two by Weber and Hummel, he mentions, as being particularly pretty, "and her manner of singing just what a lady's ought to be. No attempts at *bravuras* or graces, but all simplicity and expression." He adds that Her Royal Highness was evidently very fond of music, and would have gone on singing much longer if there had not been rather premature preparations for bed.

After breakfast the next day, he says, the Duchess having expressed a wish for a little more music, she and the Princess and himself sung together a good deal.

CHAPTER IV.

IMPORTANT AND SUGGESTIVE EVENTS.

THE PRINCESS LEARNS THE SECRET OF HER HERITAGE — FIRST STATE APPEARANCE AT QUEEN ADELAIDE'S DRAWING-ROOM—PRINCE ALBERT AS A BABY—AS A CHILD AND AS A YOUTH—THE FIRST MEETING OF PRINCESS VICTORIA AND PRINCE ALBERT.

THE Baroness Lehzen was one of the Princess Victoria's earliest guardians who remained at Court all through her youth and to whom Her Majesty was always much attached. Louise Lehzen was the daughter of a Hanoverian Clergyman, who came to England as governess to Princess Feodore Leiningen, the Queen's sister, and remained as governess to the Princess Victoria from 1824. In 1827 she was made a Hanoverian Baroness, by George IV, at the request of Princess Sophia.

From that time, Baroness Lehzen acted also as lady in attendance. On her death, so late as 1870, her old pupil recorded of her, in a passage in the Queen's Journal, which is given in the Life of the Prince Consort, " My dearest, kindest friend, old Lehzen, expired on the

9th, quite gently and peaceably.........She knew me from six months old, and, from my fifth to my eighteenth year, devoted all her care and energies to me with the most wonderful abnegation of self, never even taking one day's holiday. I adored, though I was greatly in awe of her. She really seemed to have no thought but for me............She was in her eighty-seventh year."

We are told that, even after she was married, among all the multitude of State duties, Her Majesty used to write to this dear old governess every week until, at the earnest request of the Baroness, who knew how fully the Queen's time was occupied, the letters became monthly instead of weekly.

To this lady we are indebted for an account of the way in which the great secret of her future lot was imparted to the young Princess. It is furnished in a letter which the Queen has herself placed before her subjects, and is therefore, of course, authentic.

The time of the important disclosure would be about 1831.

"I ask your Majesty's leave," wrote the Baroness, "to cite some remarkable words of your Majesty when only twelve years old, while the Regency Bill was in progress. I then said to the Duchess of Kent, that now for the first time your Majesty ought to know your place in the succession. Her Royal Highness agreed with me, and I put the genealogical table into the historical book. When Mr. Davies, (the Queen's instructor, afterwards Bishop of Peterborough) was gone, the Princess Victoria opened the book again as usual, and, seeing the additional paper, said,—

"I never saw that before."

"It was not thought necessary that you should, Princess," I answered.

"I see I am nearer the throne than I thought."

"So it is, Madam," I said.

After some moments, the Princess answered—

"Now many a child would boast, but they don't know the difficulty. There is much splendour, but there is more responsibility." The Princess having lifted up the fore-finger of her right hand while she spoke, gave me that little hand, saying, "I will be good. I understand now why you urged me so much to learn Latin. My Aunts Augusta and Mary never did; but you told me Latin is the foundation of English Grammar and of all the elegant expressions, and I learned it as you wished it; but I understand all better now." And the Princess gave me her hand, repeating, "I will be good."

I then said, "but your Aunt Adelaide is still young and may have children, and of course they would ascend the throne after their father William IV., and not you, Princess."

The Princess answered, "And if it was so, I should never feel disappointed, for I know by the love Aunt Adelaide bears me how fond she is of children."

This incident shows the future Queen in a truly noble light, as both unselfish and wise beyond her years. It is no wonder that almost every life of Her Majesty that has been written contains the story as it is given us by the Baroness Lehzen.

"In February 1831, when Princess Victoria was twelve," Miss Tytler writes, "she made her first appearance in state at the most magnificent drawing-room which had been seen since that which had taken place on the presentation of Princess Charlotte of Wales upon the occasion of her marriage.

"The drawing-room was held by Queen Adelaide, and it was to do honour to the new Queen no less than to commemorate the approaching completion of the Princess's twelfth year that the heiress to the throne was present in a prominent position, an object of the greatest interest to the splendid company. She came with the Duchess and a numerous and illustrious suite of ladies and gentlemen." Miss Tytler goes on to say, "The Princess's dress was made, as the Queen's often was afterwards, entirely of articles manufactured in the United Kingdom. She wore a frock of English blonde, 'simple, modest and becoming.' She stood on the left of Her Majesty on the throne, and 'contemplated all that passed with much dignity, but with evident interest.' We are further told, what we can well believe, that she excited general admiration as well as interest. We can without difficulty call up before us the girlish figure in its pure white dress, the soft open face, the fair hair, the candid blue eyes, the frank lips slightly apart, showing the white pearly teeth. The intelligent observation, the remarkable absence of self-consciousness and consequent power of self-control and of thought for others, which struck all who approached her in the great crisis of her history six years afterwards, were already conspicuous in the young girl."

In the Spring of 1836, the Duchess of Kent sent an invitation to her brother, the reigning Duke of Saxe-Coburg, to come and visit her with his two sons. And, accordingly, in that month which is the sweetest in many respects of all the year, in spite of inconstant skies and uncertain storms of wind and rain, when Kensington Gardens were fair with tender green foliage, chestnut and hawthorn blossoms, the father and his two sons arrived. It was not without due thought that the invitation was given and accepted, for one of the sons, Prince Albert, had long been destined by loving minds, as far as thought could do so, to be the husband of our Queen.

Born three months after the Princess Victoria, in the Rosenau, the Summer residence of the Duke of Saxe-

Coburg, and brought up at first by his grandmother, the mother of the Duchess of Kent, it was very natural that the old lady, loving both grand-children, should early desire fondly the future union of her younger charge with the "Mayflower" across the sea.

When he was two years old, she wrote to the Duchess of Kent, "Little Alberinchen, with his large blue eyes and dimpled cheeks is bewitching, forward and quick as a weasel." And again,

"The little fellow is the pendant to the pretty cousin (Princess Victoria), very handsome but too slight for a boy; lively, very funny; all good nature and full of mischief."

And, once more,

"They (Albert and Ernest his little brother) are very good boys on the whole, very obedient and easy to manage. Albert used to rebel a little sometimes, but a grave face brings the little fellow to submit. Now he obeys me at a look."

The young Prince is described as being singularly easy to instruct, and of an intellectual and thoughtful turn of character, while his love of order was conspicuous at an early age. His studies were a pleasure to him, and he had a constant love of occupation. His tutor said, "To do *something* was with him a necessity." And we are told his perseverance and application were only equalled by his facility of occupation.

His eager desire for knowledge did not, however, lessen his enjoyment of the active sports and amusements which generally have, and ought to have, so much attraction for boys. Indeed, he seems to have thrown himself into his games and bodily exercises with the same zeal and thoroughness with which he pursued his studies. In his games with his brother Ernest and his young companions his was the directing mind.

"He was always an intelligent child," writes Mr. Florschütz, "and held a certain sway over his elder brother, who rather kindly submitted to it."

In a letter of Count Mensdórf* to the Queen, he says,

"Albert; as a child, was of a mild, benevolent disposition. It was only what he thought unjust or dishonest that could make him angry. Thus I recollect one day when we were children, Albert, Ernest, Ferdinand, Augustus, Alexander, myself, and a few other boys (if I am not mistaken Paul Wangenheim was one) were playing at the Rosenau, and some of us were to storm the old ruined tower on the side of the castle, which the others were to defend. One of us suggested that there was a place at the back by which we could get in without being seen, and thus capture it without difficulty. Albert declared that "this would be most unbecoming in a Saxon knight, who should always

---

* "Early Days of the Prince Consort."

attack the enemy in front," and so we fought for the tower so honestly and vigorously, that Albert by mistake, for I was on his side, gave me a blow upon the nose, of which I still bear the mark. I need not say how sorry he was."

"Prince Albert had a natural talent for imitation and a great sense of the ludicrous, either in persons or things; but he was never severe or ill-natured. The general kindness of his disposition preventing him from pushing a joke, however much he might enjoy it, so as to hurt anyone's feelings. Every man has, more or less a ridiculous side; and to *quiz* this, in a friendly and good-humoured manner is, after all, the pleasantest description of humour. Albert possessed this rare gift in an eminent degree.

"From his earliest infancy he was distinguished for perfect moral purity, both in word and deed; and to this he owed the sweetness of disposition so much admired by every one."

A little later on, in the same letter which was written in 1863, the writer adds,

"Some time ago I collected all the letters I have of dearest Albert's, and, in one of them I found a passage most characteristic of his noble way of thinking, as shown and maintained by him from his earliest childhood.

"'The poor soldiers,' he says, 'always do their duty

in the most brilliant manner, but as soon as matters come again into the hands of politicians and diplomats, everything is again spoiled and confused. Oxenstiern's saying to his son may still be quoted: "My son, when you look at things more closely, you will be surprised with how little wisdom the world is governed." I should like to add, 'and with how little morality.'"

How much those words contain! We again see the Saxon knight, who as a child declared that you must attack your enemy in front, who hates every crooked path; and, on the other hand, the noble heart which feels deeply the misfortune of a government not guided by reason and morality.

The little hero of the fortress showed his kindness of heart, too, at the early age of six years, for, having seen a poor man's cottage burnt to the ground, he never rested until a sufficient sum of money had been collected to rebuild the ruined edifice.

But to return to the grandmother's idea of the marriage between the Cousins, the Prince used to relate that "when he was a child of three years old his nurse always told him that he should marry the Queen, and that when he first thought of marrying at all, he always thought of her."

But all this might have come to nothing if it had not been for King Leopold, who, as the children grew up, warmly encouraged the idea. He was deeply attached to his niece, and he loved his younger nephew at Coburg as if he were his son.

We are told that Prince Albert was, as a young man, handsome, clever and good, endowed with all winning attributes, with wise well-balanced judgment in advance of his years, and, though of earnest steadfast purpose, he possessed a gentle sympathetic temper and a merry humour. Where could King Leopold find a better suitor for the future Queen of England?

It was necessary that if the desired favourable impression should be made, the young couple should meet each other. But, while the opportunity should be given them, it was settled that the underlying motive for their meeting should be concealed, "that they might be perfectly at ease with one another."

And so the invitation was given and accepted, and in about a month, as we have said, Prince Albert arrived at Kensington with his father and brother. History does not tell us how the Royal cousins met, and whether some half secret emotion dimmed the two pairs of blue eyes which then encountered each other for the first time.

Her Majesty has herself at a later date recorded her impressions of the visit. She says,

"The Prince was at that time shorter than his brother, already very handsome, but very stout, and which he entirely grew out of afterwards. He was most

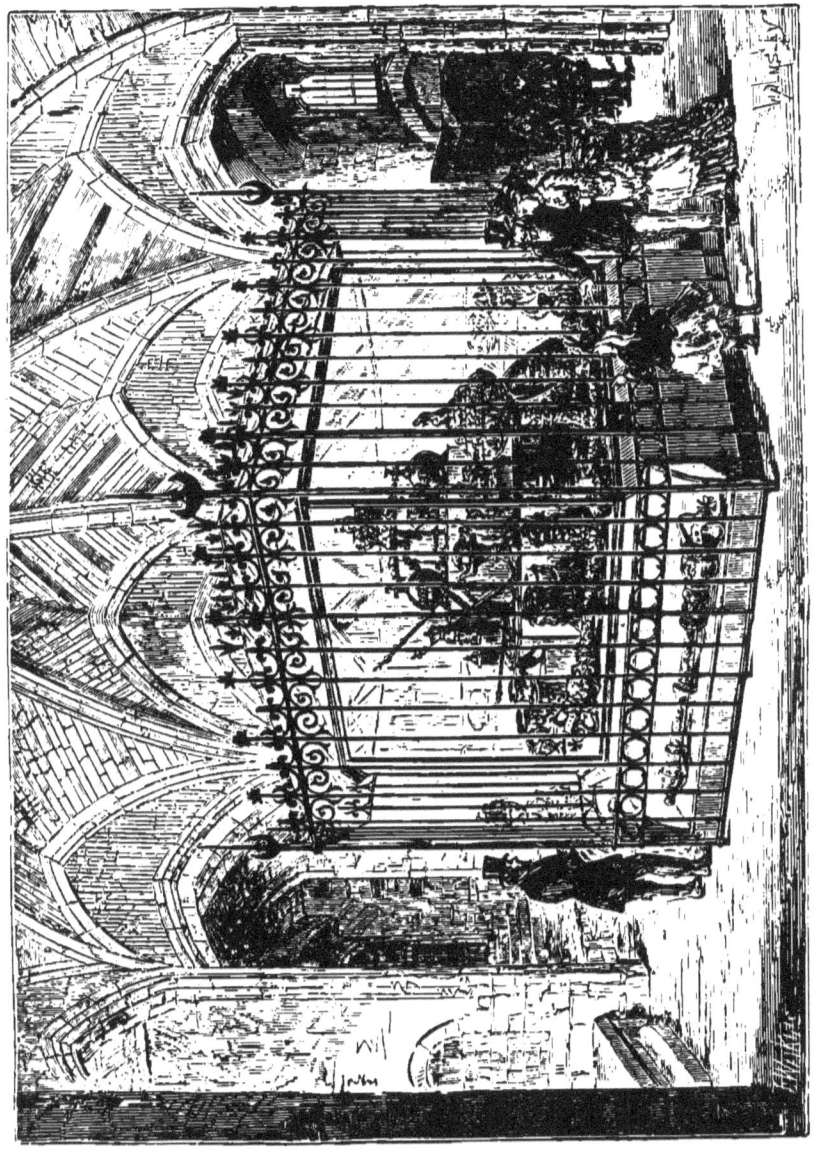

THE CROWN JEWELS, TOWER OF LONDON.

amiable, natural, unaffected and merry :—full of interest in everything—playing on the Piano with the Princess, his cousin — drawing; in short, ever occupied. He always paid the greatest attention to all he saw, and the Queen remembers well how intently he listened to the sermon preached in St. Paul's, when he and his father and brother accompanied the Duchess of Kent and the Princess there, on the occasion of the service attended by the children of the different charity schools. It is indeed rare to see a Prince, not seventeen years of age, bestowing such earnest attention on a sermon."*

The visit lasted about a month, and the cousins shared, as we have seen, their favourite pursuits music and drawing together, Prince Albert accompanying the Princess on the piano and drawing and singing with her.

We can easily understand "it was a happy and busy time, though some of the late dinners, at which the Prince drank only water, were doubtless dull enough to the young people, and Prince Albert, accustomed to the early hours and simple habits of Germany, felt the change trying. He confessed that it was sometimes with difficulty he kept awake."

At the end of the month, the Prince went away to study diligently with his brother at Brussels and Bonn. And when King Leopold could no longer refrain from

* "Memorandum by the Queen."

expressing his hopes, his Royal niece returned him the most satisfactory answer.

"I have only now to beg you, my dearest uncle," she wrote, "to take care of the health of one now so dear to me, and to take him under your special protection. I hope and trust that all will now go on prosperously and well on this subject, now of so much importance to me."

An affectionate correspondence was begun and carried on for a year, but no further communication, we are told, was made to the Prince as to the feelings he had excited.

CHAPTER V.

THE ACCESSION.

QUEEN VICTORIA—HER MAJESTY'S FIRST PRIVY COUNCIL—PROCLAMATION OF THE QUEEN—HER MAJESTY'S EMOTION—HER DESIRE TO BE ALONE FOR A SHORT TIME.

ON the 20th of June, 1837, a little party of gentlemen, consisting of the Archbishop of Canterbury, Dr. Hawley, the Lord Chamberlain, the Marquis of Conyngham, the Earl of Albemarle, the Master of the Horse, and Sir Henry Halford, (the late King's Physician), started to ride from Windsor to Kensington.

All through the Summer night these solemn and stately gentlemen rode on, occasionally nodding with fatigue or exchanging remarks about the late reign (for King William had died just before they started, at two o'clock that morning), and uttering predictions of what might happen in the one which was just about opening.

A little before five, "when the birds were already in full chorus in Kensington Gardens," the party stood at the main door of the palace demanding admittance.

That was granted none too readily. For Miss Wynne tells us in her "*Diary of a Lady of Quality*,"

"They knocked, they rang, they thumped for a considerable time before they could rouse the porter at the gate. They were again kept waiting in the courtyard, then turned into one of the lower rooms, where they seemed forgotten by everybody. They rang the bell and desired that the attendant of the Princess Victoria might be sent to inform Her Royal Highness that they requested an audience on business of importance. After another delay and another ringing to enquire the cause, the attendant was summoned, who stated that the Princess was in such a sweet sleep that she could not venture to disturb her.

Then they said, "We are come on business of State to the Queen, and even her sleep must give way to that."

It did; and to prove that she did not keep them waiting, in a few minutes she came into the room in a loose white night-gown and shawl, her night-cap thrown off, and her hair falling upon her shoulders, her feet in slippers, tears in her eyes, but perfectly collected and dignified."

The first request of the Queen, we are told, on being informed of her new dignity was made to the Archbishop.

"I ask your prayers on my behalf," she said, and

they knelt together, while the young Queen "inaugurated her reign, like the young King of Israel in the olden time, by asking from the Most High, who ruleth over the kingdoms of men, an understanding heart to judge so great a people."

The first act of Her Majesty's life as Queen was also exceedingly beautiful.

The Marquess of Conyngham was the bearer to the Queen of a request from the Queen-dowager that she might remain at Windsor until after the funeral. In reply, the Queen wrote an affectionate and tender letter of condolence to her aunt, begging her only to consult her own health and convenience, and to stay at Windsor as long as she pleased.

Her Majesty having finished her letter, addressed it as usual to The Queen of England.

A bystander, probably one of the ladies-in-waiting, observing this, interposed,

"Your Majesty, *you* are Queen of England."

"Yes," was the considerate reply of the young Queen, "but the widowed Queen is not to be reminded of the fact first by me."

A Privy Council was held as soon as possible at Kensington Palace. And it must have been very formidable for the eighteen-year-old Queen. Did her thoughts wander to the young student, we wonder, who was studying quietly at the time, at a little University town on the Rhine? Would it not have been natural for her to wish he were at her side with his clear judgment and sympathising friendship for herself? History does not tell us. We are only given a glimpse of a slight girlish figure in simple mourning occupying her position at the head of the Council-table and occupying it well.

The Duke of Wellington wrote, "As soon as I heard that King William had expired, I hurried to Kensington, to be present at the first council of the new sovereign. This I think was the most interesting scene I have ever witnessed..........I am quite in raptures with the deportment of the young Queen, nothing could be more exquisitely proper. She looked modest, sorrowful, dejected, diffident, but at the same time she was quite cool and collected, and composed and firm. Her childish appearance was gone. She was an intelligent and graceful young woman, capable of acting and thinking for herself. Considering that she was the only female in the room, and that she had no one about her with whom she was familiar, no human being was ever placed in a more trying situation."

When the Princes, Peers and other Councillors met, they signed the oath of allegiance, and were all sworn in members of the Council, and then Her Majesty addressed them,

'If the millions," said Harriet Martineau, "who

longed to know how the young Sovereign looked and felt, could have heard her first address, it would have gone far to satisfy them. The address was, of course, prepared for her; but the manner and voice were her own, and they told much. Her manner was composed, modest and dignified, her voice firm and sweet; her reading, as usual, beautiful. She took the necessary oaths, and received the eager homage of the thronging nobility without agitation or any awkwardness. The declaration contained an affectionate reference to the deceased King; an assertion of her attachment to the country; and of her intention to rule in accordance with it; a grateful allusion to her mother's educational care of her; an avowal that, under circumstances of such imminent responsibility as hers, she relied for support and guidance on Divine Providence, and a pledge that her life should be devoted to the happiness of her people. The Ministers returned unto her hands, and received again, the seals of their respective offices; the stamps in official use were ordered to be altered, as also the prayers of the Church which related to the Royal Family. The Proclamation was prepared and signed by the Privy Councillors, and the Queen appointed the next day, Wednesday, for the ceremony."

Mr. Greville's comment on the scene was singularly enthusiastic for such a man, "Never," he said, "was anything like the impression she produced, or the chorus of praise and admiration which is raised about her manner and behaviour and certainly not without justice. It was very extraordinary and something far beyond what was looked for. Her extreme youth and inexperience, and the ignorance of the world concerning her, naturally excited intense curiosity to see how she would act on this trying occasion: and there was a considerable assemblage at the Palace, notwithstanding the short notice which was given. The first thing to be done was to teach her her lesson, which, for this purpose, Melbourne had himself to learn......... She bowed to the lords, took her seat and then read her speech in a clear distinct and audible voice, without any appearance of fear or embarrassment. She was quite plainly dressed, and in mourning. After she had read her speech, and taken and signed the oath for the security of the Church of Scotland, the Privy Councillors were sworn, the two Royal Dukes first by themselves; and as these two old men, her uncles, knelt before her, swearing allegiance and kissing her hand, I saw her blush up to the eyes, as if she felt the contrast between their civil and their natural relations, and this was the only sign of emotion which she evinced. Her manner to them was very graceful and engaging; she kissed them both, and rose from her chair and moved towards the Duke of Sussex, who was furthest from her, and too infirm to reach her. She seemed rather bewildered at the multitude of men who were sworn, and who came one after another to kiss her hand, but she did not speak to anybody, nor did she make the slightest difference in her manner, or show any in her countenance, to any individual of any rank, station or party."

But we are told by Gilchrist that she would not let her Uncle, the Duke of Sussex, who was sixty-four, kiss her hand, but when she kissed his cheek instead, she said, "Do not kneel, my Uncle, for I am still Victoria, your niece."

"I particularly watched her," Greville went on, "when Melbourne and the Ministers and the Duke of Wellington and Peel approached her. She went through the whole ceremony, occasionally looking to Melbourne for instruction when she had any doubt what to do, which hardly ever occurred, with perfect calmness and self-possession, but at the same time with a graceful modesty and propriety, particularly interesting and ingratiating."

On the next day, June 21st, the Princess Victoria was formally proclaimed Queen of Great Britain and Ireland, from St. James's Palace. Long before the hour fixed for the ceremony, all the avenues to the palace were crowded, besides all the balconies, windows and every elevated position.

Ladies and gentlemen congregated in the quadrangle in front of the window at which Her Majesty was to appear, while even the parapets above were filled with people. We are told the great Irish agitator O'Connel, in the front line opposite the windows attracted considerable attention by waving his hat and cheering most vehemently.

The scene which the spectators alone presented must have been a very imposing one. At ten o'clock the guns in the park fired a salute, and, immediately afterwards, the Queen appeared, standing between Lord Melbourne and Lord Lansdowne, at the window of the Presence Chamber. Her mother stood close behind her, and, while the Queen was greeted with deafening cheers, she also received most cordial applause.

Her Majesty looked fatigued and pale, but returned the repeated cheers with remarkable ease and dignity. She was dressed in deep mourning, with a white tippet, white cuffs, and a border of white lace under a small black bonnet, which was placed far back on her head exhibiting her light hair in front simply parted over her forehead. Her Majesty seemed to view the proceedings with considerable interest, as, also, did the Duchess of Kent. As Her Majesty appeared at the window the band of the Royal Guards struck up the National Anthem. On its conclusion, Sir William

Wood, acting for the Garter Knight-at-arms, read aloud the Proclamation, as follows,

* "Whereas it has pleased Almighty God to call to His mercy our late Sovereign lord, King William the Fourth, of blessed and glorious memory, by whose decease the imperial crown of the United Kingdom of Great Britain and Ireland is solely and rightfully come to the high and mighty Princess Alexandrina Victoria (saving the rights of any issue of his late Majesty King William the Fourth which may be born of his late Majesty's Consort); we, therefore, the lords spiritual and temporal of this realm, being here assisted with those of his late Majesty's Privy Council, with numbers of others, principally gentlemen of quality, with the Lord Mayor, Aldermen, and citizens of London, do now hereby, with one voice and consent of tongue and heart, publish and proclaim that the high and mighty Princess Alexandrina Victoria is now, by the death of our late Sovereign of happy memory, become our only lawful and rightful liege lady, Victoria, by the grace of God Queen of the United Kingdom of Great Britain and Ireland, Defender of the Faith, saving as aforesaid: to whom, saving as aforesaid, we do acknowledge all faith and constant obedience, with all hearty and humble affection, beseeching God, by whom kings do reign, to bless the royal Princess Victoria with long and happy years to reign over us. God save the Queen!"

* Her Majesty stood at the Presence Chamber window throughout the reading of the Proclamation, during which there was considerable movement among the crowd, who would cheer and cry "God save the Queen," until Daniel O'Connel's stentorian voice commanded "Silence!"

At the termination of this proclamation, the band struck up the National Anthem, and a signal was given for the Park and Tower guns to fire. The air was rent by the loudest acclamations on all sides. "It was a little too much," we are told, "for the self-controlled young Queen, who turned to her mother, and throwing her arms about her wept without restraint."

The sight of Her Majesty's tears awoke within the people that tender regard with which the Queen is most honoured, and drew from the pen of Mrs. (then Miss Elizabeth Barret) Browning, the following lines,—

> "O maiden, heir of Kings,
>   A king has left his place,
> The Majesty of death has swept
>   All other from his face;
> And thou upon thy mother's breast
>   No longer lean adown,
> But take the glory for the rest,
> And rule the land that loves thee best.
>   The maiden wept,
>   She wept to wear a crown.

---

* From the Life of Queen Victoria.

God save thee, weeping Queen!
  Thou shalt be well beloved;
The tyrant's sceptre cannot move
  As those pure tears have moved!
The nature in thy eyes we see
  Which tyrants cannot own,
The love that guardeth liberties,
Strange blessing on the nation lies,
  Whose sovereign wept—
Yea, wept to wear a crown.

God bless thee, weeping Queen,
  With blessings more Divine;
And fill with better love than earth's
  That tender heart of thine;
That when the throne of earth shall be
  As low as graves brought down,
A piercèd hand may give to thee
The crown which angels shout to see:
  Thou wilt not weep
To wear that heavenly crown!"

"A maiden Queen in her first youth, wearing the crown and wielding the sceptre had become *un fait accompli*," Miss Tytler writes, "and the news spread over the length and breadth of the land. We have seen how it touched the oldest statesmen, to whom state ceremonials had become hackneyed—who were perhaps a little sceptical of virtue in high places."

And if it touched them, how much more likely it would be to thrill all the romantic, sensitive young hearts in the kingdom. In the person of the Queen it seemed as if womanhood and girlhood were exalted, "as if a new era must be inaugurated with such a reign, and every man worthy of the name would rally round this Una on the throne."

Yet that the Queen was, through it all, a very girl, who was almost overwhelmed now that the responsibility which, even as a little thoughtful child, she had recognised as attached to the wearer of the crown, was indeed coming upon her, we can plainly see by the emotion which overcame her more than once on that trying day.

We are told that as soon as Her Majesty found herself able to withdraw from all the duties of the solemn ceremonial, she went hastily to her mother's apartment, and there again wept as she threw herself into her arms. The Duchess tenderly soothed her, and then the Queen said,

"I can scarcely believe, Mamma, that I am Queen of England; but I suppose I really am so—am I not?"

"You know, my love, you are. You have just left a scene which must have assured you of it."

"And in time," replied Her Majesty, "I shall become accustomed to my change of character; meanwhile since it really is so, and you see in your little daughter the Sovereign of this great country, will you grant her the first request she has had occasion in her regal

THE ROYAL FAMILY.   63

capacity to put to you? I wish, my dear Mamma, to be left for two hours alone."

The Duchess understood the reason for this request, and for the first day in her daughter's life she allowed her to be left alone. The young Queen desired in human solitude, but in the presence of her Maker, to commune with herself upon the duties which would now lie before her, day after day, and year after year, as the monarch of a great and powerful empire.

CHAPTER VI.

THE YOUNG QUEEN.

LEAVING KENSINGTON FOR BUCKINGHAM PALACE—GOING TO DISSOLVE PARLIAMENT—THE DUKE OF WELLINGTON BRINGING THE FIRST DEATH WARRANT FOR HER MAJESTY TO SIGN—THE QUEEN'S REVERENCE FOR THE LORD'S DAY—REPROVING HER LADY FOR UNPUNCTUALITY—LETTER FROM PRINCE ALBERT.

ON the 13th of July, the Queen and her mother left Kensington and went to reside at Buckingham Palace. Her Majesty felt some natural grief at leaving the home of her childhood, and, we need scarcely add, her doing so was "greatly to the regret of the inhabitants."

The poor people, whose lives had been brightened by visits from the beloved Princess, must have missed her terribly.

One of these cottagers was an old soldier, who had been a servant of the Duke of Kent. The Duchess and Princess Victoria often used to visit the family in which there were two children in delicate health. The little boy died, but the girl lived and was an

HER ROYAL HIGHNESS THE PRINCESS OF WALES.

THE ROYAL FAMILY.

invalid. Not long after Her Majesty had left Kensington, a clergyman calling to see this girl found her very cheerful. Putting her hand under her pillow, she drew forth a book of Psalms, saying,

"Look there! See what the new Queen has sent me to-day, by one of her ladies, with a message. She says that though now Queen of England, as she had to leave Kensington, she did not forget me."

The lady had also told the girl that the figures marked upon the margin were the dates when the Queen herself used to read the psalms marked, and that the marker with the peacock worked on it was made by the Queen.

The girl, bursting into tears, after telling the clergyman this, added, "Was it not beautiful, Sir?"

Miss Tytler gives us a glimpse of the way in which the young Queen left Kensington,

"Shortly after one o'clock an escort of Lancers took up a position on the Palace Green, long previous to which, an immense concourse of respectable persons had thronged the avenue and every open space near the Palace.

"About half-past one an open carriage, drawn by four greys, preceded by two outriders and followed by an open barouche drawn by four bays, drove up from Her Majesty's Mews, Pimlico, and stopped before the grand entrance to the Duchess of Kent's apartments.

The Queen, accompanied by the Duchess of Kent and Baroness Lehzen, almost immediately got into the first carriage. There was a tumult of cheering, frankly acknowledged. It is said that the Queen looked 'pale and a little sad' at the parting moment."

Was she thinking of the responsibilites, we wonder, which all these changes were betokening to her thoughtful mind, was she resolving again, as she had resolved so long ago, that, however hard the work would be, and however heavy the burden, she would be *good* and would do that which was right in the sight of God and man? We can easily imagine it.

And so, as the carriage dashed away in a whirl of July dust, leaving the familiar Palace Green, with its spreading trees, behind, we will turn to other scenes.

Her Majesty's first Court levée was held soon after her arrival at Buckingham Palace, and it was a very splendid affair. The young Queen was richly dressed; her head glittering with diamonds, and the insignia of the Garter and other orders blazing on her breast. "She seemed already to have increased in grace and brilliancy, and every one was delighted with her."

Two days later the Queen went in state to dissolve Parliament. The carriage with the eight cream-coloured horses, which are so dear to the London populace, was used. The Queen was accompanied by the Earl of Albemarle, Master of the Horse, and the Countess of Mulgrave, the Lady-in-waiting. Other carriages with other ladies and gentlemen also followed, and the streets were lined, while the house-tops were covered with spectators whose cheers were deafening. On stopping at the House of Lords, Her Majesty was received by a Battalion of the Grenadier Guards, whose splendid band played the National Anthem.

Her Majesty, who was attired in a splendid white satin robe, with the ribbon of the Garter crossing her shoulder, a magnificent tiara of diamonds on her head, and a necklace and stomacher of large and costly brilliants, entered the old Houses of Parliament and seated herself on the Throne of her ancestors.

The usual formalities having been gone through, the Queen read her speech from the throne, in which she thanked the Parliament for its condolence upon the death of the late King, and for its expression of attachment and affection for herself; announced her intention to preserve all rights civil as well as spiritual; and, after touching on the usual topics relating to home and foreign affairs, ended with the words;—

"I ascend the throne with a deep sense of the responsibility which is imposed upon me; but I am supported by the consciousness of my own right intentions, and by my dependence upon the protection of God Almighty. It will be my care to strengthen our institutions, civil and ecclesiastical, by making discreet improvement wherever it is required, and to do all in my power to compose and allay animosity and discord. Acting upon these principles, I shall upon all occasions look with confidence to the wisdom of Parliament and the affections of my people, which form the true support of the Crown and ensure the stability of the Constitution."

Her Majesty read the speech deliberately and with a sweet voice which was heard all over the House, while she was distinguished by her natural grace and self-possession.

Fanny Kemble, who was present, thus wrote concerning the principal object of the striking historic scene,

"The Queen was not handsome, but very pretty, and the singularity of her great position lent a sentimental and poetical charm to her youthful face and figure. The serene, serious sweetness of her candid brow and clear soft eyes gave dignity to the girlish countenance; while the want of height only added to the effect of extreme youth of the round but slender person, and gracefully moulded hands and arms. The Queen's voice was exquisite, nor have I ever heard any spoken words more musical in their gentle distinctness than, 'My Lords and Gentlemen,' which broke the breathless silence of the illustrious assembly, whose gaze was riveted on that fair flower of royalty. The enunciation was as perfect as the intonation was melodious, and I think it is impossible to hear a more excellent utterance than that of the Queen's English by the English Queen."

Not long after that, Her Majesty was called upon to sign her first death-warrant. The Duke of Wellington presented it to her, and it concerned a deserter who had been condemned to death by Court Martial.

"Have you nothing to say on behalf of this man?" asked the young Queen, her blue eyes filling with tears.

"Nothing; he has deserted three times," replied the iron Duke.

"Oh, your Grace, think again!"

"Well, your Majesty," said the brave veteran, "though he is certainly a very bad *soldier*, some witnesses spoke for his character, and, for ought I know to the contrary, he may be a good *man*."

"Oh, thank you for that a thousand times!" exclaimed the Queen; and writing "pardoned" on the paper, she pushed it across the table to the Duke, her hand trembling with emotion.

We are told an interesting story of her Majesty's respect for the Divinely appointed day of rest.

Late one Saturday night a Minister arrived at Windsor on State business.

"I have brought down for your Majesty's inspection some documents of great importance," he said. "But as I shall be obliged to trouble you to examine them in detail, I will not encroach on the time of your Majesty to-night, but will request your attention to-morrow morning."

"To-morrow morning," said the Queen, "to-morrow is Sunday, my Lord."

"True, your Majesty, but business of the State will not admit of delay."

"I am aware of that," replied the Queen, "and as your lordship could not have arrived earlier at the Palace to-night, I will, if these letters are of such pressing importance, attend to their contents to-morrow morning."

Next morning the Queen and the Court went to Church, and so did the noble lord; and the subject of the sermon was, "The Christian Sabbath; its duties and obligations."

"How did your lordship like the sermon?" enquired the Queen of the Minister afterwards.

"Very much indeed, your Majesty," he replied.

"Well then I will not conceal from you," said Her Majesty, "that last night I sent the clergyman the text from which he preached. I hope we shall all be improved by the sermon."

Nothing more was said about the papers all day, but when the Queen wished the minister good night, she said,

"To-morrow morning, my Lord, at any hour you

please; as early as seven, my Lord, if you like, we will look into those papers."

"I could not think of intruding upon your Majesty at so early an hour," replied the Minister, "nine o'clock will be quite soon enough."

Accordingly at nine o'clock the next day the Queen was ready to confer with her Minister about the papers.

Though very kind and considerate, Her Majesty was particular about the way in which her household was conducted. We are told a story which, while showing this, lets us see also how pleasant the Queen was, even while so young, to those who were about her.

A certain noble lady, who had been appointed to a place of great distinction about the Royal person, was not very punctual, at first, in her hours of official duty. On the second or third morning that this occurred Her Majesty received her noble attendant with her watch in her hand.

"I am afraid I have unfortunately been the occasion of detaining your Majesty," observed her ladyship, apologetically.

"Yes, full ten minutes," was the grave reply, "and I beg this want of punctuality may not occur again."

Then, seeing that, in the agitation caused by this reproof, the lady experienced some embarrassment in the arrangement of her shawl, Her Majesty showed that no unkind feeling had prompted her remark by condescending to assist her with her own hands, observing with much sweetness as she did so,

"We shall all become more perfect in our duties in time, I hope."

When the news of Queen Victoria's accession became known to Prince Albert, who was then a student at Bonn, he wrote to Her Majesty, as follows,—

"Now you are Queen of the mightiest land of Europe, in your hand lies the happiness of millions. May Heaven assist you and strengthen you with its strength in that high but difficult task. I hope that your reign may be long, happy and glorious, and that your efforts may be rewarded by the thankfulness and love of your subjects."

The Prince was strongly averse to putting himself forward in any way, and it was determined by the friends of both the young people that, lest too hasty a report of their possible engagement might be made, Prince Albert should travel for some months. Accompanied by his brother, he accordingly did so through Switzerland and Northern Italy.

CHAPTER VII.

THE CORONATION.

PRELIMINARY ARRANGEMENTS—CROWDING OF LADIES AND GENTLEMEN TO THE ABBEY IN THE EARLY MORNING—THE ROYAL PROCESSION—THE CORONATION—LORD ROLLE'S DISASTER—RETURN FROM THE ABBEY—LITTLE DASH.

A YEAR after the Proclamation of the Queen, the ceremony of the Coronation took place in Westminster Abbey. This had been looked forward to most eagerly on all sides, and some conception of the magnificence of the occasion may be gathered from the fact that the expense of the Coronation was £70,000, that it was computed that the public paid £200,000 for seats to view the procession, and that not less than 400,000 persons visited the metropolis to witness the ceremony.

Amongst the proclamations issued, was one declaring it to be the Queen's royal will and pleasure at her approaching Coronation to dispense with the ceremonies usually performed in Westminster Hall on such an occasion. One of these ceremonies was the entry of the Champion of England on horseback, whose right it was to throw down his gauntlet in defence of the Sovereign, challenging any one to take it up.

Another ancient custom which was to be dispensed with was that the peers should do homage by kissing the left cheek of the Sovereign. This, in the case of six hundred spiritual and temporal Peers, would have been a truly appaling prospect for the girl-Queen if it had been persisted in.

"The crown in which the Queen was to appear at the Coronation was made and exhibited by Messrs. Rundell and Bridge. It was," Mr. Smith tells us, "more tasteful than that worn by George IV. and William IV., which had been broken up. The old crown weighed more than seven pounds, and the new one, which was smaller, only about three pounds. It was composed of hoops of silver, enclosing a cap of deep blue velvet; the hoops were completely covered with precious stones, surmounted by a ball covered with small diamonds, and having a Maltese cross of brilliants on the top of it. The cross had in its centre a splendid sapphire; the rim of the crown was clustered with brilliants, and ornamented with *fleur-de-lis* and Maltese crosses, equally rich. In the front of the large Maltese cross was the enormous heart-shaped ruby which had been worn by Edward the Black Prince, and which afterwards figured in the helmet of Henry V. at the battle of Agincourt. Beneath this, in the circular rim, was a large oblong sapphire. There were many other precious gems, emeralds, rubies, and sapphires, and several small clusters of drop pearls. The lower part of the jewels on the crown was estimated at £112,760."

The Coronation day was the 28th of June. London was very early awake, and by six o'clock in the morning, carriages and foot-passengers were pouring into the West end. From Hyde Park corner to the Abbey scarcely a house was without a scaffolding which was soon filled with sight-seers. Seats fetched a high price, whilst, on the eve of the ceremony, tickets for the interior of the Abbey were bought for more than twenty guineas each.

Harriet Martineau wrote,—

"The maids called me at half-past two that June morning, mistaking the clock—I slept no more, and rose at half-past three. As I began to dress the twenty-one guns were fired, which must have wakened all the sleepers in London. When the maid came to dress me she said numbers of ladies were already hurrying to the Abbey. I saw the grey old Abbey from the window as I dressed, and thought what would have gone forward within it before the sun set upon it. My mother had laid out her pearl ornaments for me. The feeling was very strange of dressing in crape, blonde, and pearls at five in the morning"—But when Miss Martineau arrived she found, "except a mere sprinkling of oddities, every body was in full dress. In the whole assemblage I counted six bonnets. The scarlet of the military officers mixed in well, and the groups of the clergy were dignified; but to an unaccustomed eye the prevalence of Court-dresses had a curious effect. I was perpetually taking whole groups of gentlemen for quakers till I recollected myself. The Earl-marshal's assistants, called Gold Sticks, looked well from above, lightly fluttering about in white breeches, silk stockings, blue-laced frocks and white sashes. The throne——an armchair with a round back, covered, as was its footstool, with cloth of gold—stood on an elevation of four steps in the centre of the area. The first Peeress took her seat in the north transept opposite, at a quarter before seven, and three of the Bishops came next. From that time the peers and their ladies arrived faster and faster. Each Peeress was conducted by two Gold Sticks, one of whom handed her to her seat, and the other bore and arranged her train on her lap, and saw that her coronet footstool and book were comfortably placed............... About nine the first gleams of the sun slanted into the Abbey and presently travelled down to the Peeresses. I had never before seen the full effect of diamonds. As the light travelled each Peeress shone like a rainbow. The brightness, vastness, splendour and dreamy magnificence of the scene produced a strange effect of exhaustion and sleepiness."

At ten o'clock a salute of twenty-one guns, and the hoisting of the imperial standard, in front of the palace, announced the fact that Her Majesty had entered the state carriage, with its eight cream-coloured horses. The Mistress of the Robes and the Master of the Horse accompanied Her Majesty. The procession set forth preceded by trumpeters and Life Guards. Then came the foreign ministers and ambassadors, followed by the carriages of the Royal Family, containing the Duchess of Kent, the Duchess of Gloucester, the Duke and Duchess of Cambridge and the Duke of Sussex. Next Her Majesty's carriages containing the members of her household and others, and then, after officers and guards, her own State coach, surmounted by its gold crown. The procession was followed by Life Guards.

"The earth was alive with men," wrote one spectator, ..."the windows were lifted out of their frames;" so that, regardless of the exposure of their homes to the public gaze, all might be able to see as much as possible of the great sight of the day.

The weather was not promising. For the season of the year it was cold, and some rain fell; but the shower ceased, and the day turned out fresh and bright, "with sunshine gilding the darkest cloud."

Her Majesty, we are told, appeared in excellent spirits and highly delighted with the imposing scene. The troops saluted in succession as she passed, and remained with presented arms until the royal carriage had passed the front of each battalion, the bands continuing to play the National Anthem.

We are told, too, that every window along the route was a bouquet, every balcony a parterre of living loveliness and beauty; and, as the Queen passed, scarfs, handkerchiefs and flowers were waved with the most boisterous enthusiasm.

Her Majesty was more than once visibly affected by these exhilarating demonstrations, and occasionally turned to the Duchess of Sutherland to conceal or express her emotion.

At half-past eleven the guns told that the Queen had arrived, but as much had to be done in the robing-room, it was a long time before she appeared in the Abbey.

A little after twelve the grand procession of the day entered the choir. A platform had been raised there, under the central tower of the Abbey and covered with a carpet of cloth of gold and upon it the chair of homage superbly gilt. Further on within the chancel, near the altar, was Edward the Confessor's chair. The altar was covered with massive gold plate.

The procession was headed by the prebendaries and

Dean of Westminster, followed by the great officers of Her Majesty's household. Then the Lord Privy Seal, the Lord President of the Council, the Lord Chancellor of Ireland, the Archbishop of Armagh, the Archbishop of York, the Lord Chancellor of England and the Archbishop of Canterbury, came next. And then the Princesses of the Blood Royal, the Duchess of Cambridge wearing a robe of estate of purple velvet and wearing a circlet of gold, her train being borne by Lady Caroline Campbell and her coronet by Viscount Villiers; and the Duchess of Kent, in a robe of estate of purple velvet and wearing a circlet of gold, with her train borne by the hapless Lady Flora Hastings and her coronet by Viscount Emlyn. Next came the Regalia—St. Edward's staff borne by the Duke of Roxburge, the golden spurs by Lord Byron; the sceptre with the cross by the Duke of Cleveland, the sword of mercy by the Duke of Devonshire; the second sword by the Duke of Sutherland; and the third sword by the Marquis of Westminster. Black Rod and Deputy-Garter walked before Lord Willoughby D'Eresby, Lord Great Chamberlain of England, with Page and Coronet.

The Princes of the blood Royal followed, the Duke of Cambridge in his robes and carrying his baton, as Field Marshal; and the Duke of Sussex also in his robes of state. The High Constables of Ireland and Scotland followed. The Earl Marshal of England,

Viscount Melbourne bearing the sword of State, the Lord High Constable of England, the Duke of Wellington, with his staff and baton as Field-Marshal, attended by two pages. The sceptre with the dove, borne by the Duke of Richmond, page and coronet; St. Edward's crown borne by the Lord High Steward, the Duke of Hamilton, attended by two pages; the orb borne by the Duke of Somerset, page and coronet. The patina borne by the Bishop of Bangor; the Bible, borne by the Bishop of Winchester, and the chalice, borne by the Bishop of London.

At last the Queen entered, walking between the Bishops of Bath and Wells and Durham, with Gentlemen-at-Arms on each side. She was not nineteen years of age, with a fair pleasant face, slight figure, rather small in stature, but "showing a queenly carriage, especially in the pose of the throat and head. She wore a Royal robe of crimson velvet, furred with ermine and bordered with gold lace. She had on, also, the collars of her Orders, with a circlet of gold upon her head. Her train was borne by eight "beautiful young ladies," the daughters of noblemen of high rank in the peerage, some of whom officiated again, later on, as the Queen's bridesmaids. Other distinguished ladies and high officials followed.

The scene was so brilliant, we are told, when the Queen entered the choir that it was almost over-

St. George's Chapel, Windsor.

whelming. The Turkish ambassador, who was absolutely bewildered, stopped in astonishment, and, for some time, would not move to his allotted place.

As the Queen advanced slowly towards the centre of the choir, she was received with hearty plaudits, everybody rising, the anthem "*I was glad when they said unto me, Let us go into the house of the Lord,*" was then sung by musicians. Then, with thrilling effect and trumpet accompaniment, "God save the Queen," was rendered. Meanwhile guns boomed outside, and the young Queen moved towards a chair placed midway between the chair of homage and the altar on the carpeted space before described. Here Her Majesty knelt for a short time in silent prayer. Her mind must have been agitated with deep and contending emotions; and there were many who shed tears at the sight of her kneeling there, the centre of so much splendour and the cynosure of a great empire, to implore the Divine aid in the fulfilment of her tremendous sovereign duties.

When Her Majesty rose from her knees she took her seat in the chair and the ceremony proceeded. The pealing notes of the Anthem rang through the arches of the Abbey, and scarcely had the music ceased when the Westminster scholars (in pursuance of their prescriptive right) rose and shouted, in almost deafening chorus, "Victoria, Victoria! *Vivat Victoria Regina!*"

The Archbishop of Canterbury now came forward,

accompanied by the Lord Chancellor, Lord Chamberlain, the Lord High Constable and the Earl Marshal, and preceded by the Deputy Garter, and presenting the young Queen to her people said,—

"Sirs, I here present unto you Queen Victoria, the undoubted Queen of this realm, wherefore all you who are come this day to do your homage, are you willing to do the same?"

To this there was a rapturous and general shout of "God save Queen Victoria."

The Archbishop turning to the north, south and west sides of the Abbey repeated, "God save Queen Victoria," the Queen remaining standing and turning about to face her loyal lieges on each side as their acclamations rent the air. Then the drums beat, the trumpets sounded and the band struck up the National Anthem. This part of the ceremonial has been described as the most striking and most picturesque.

The Bishops who bore the patina, Bible and Chalice, now placed the same on the altar. There, soon afterwards, the Queen, having advanced to the altar, made her first offering, a pall or altar cloth of gold, delivering it to the Archbishop of Canterbury who placed it upon the altar. And, next, an ingot of gold of one pound weight being presented to the Queen by the Lord Great Chamberlain, Her Majesty delivered it to the Archbishop by whom it was put into the oblation basin.

After prayer and the Communion service conducted by the Archbishop and two Bishops, the Bishop of London preached the sermon from 2nd Chronicles xxxiv. 31.

"*And the King stood in his place, and made a covenant before the Lord, to walk after the Lord, and to keep His Commandments, and His testimonies, and His statutes, with all his heart, and with all his soul, to perform the words of the covenant which are written in this book.*"

In the course of the sermon the Bishop spoke highly of the unfeigned religion of the late King and exhorted his youthful successor to follow in his footsteps. Her Majesty paid great attention to the sermon, and when her dead uncle was mentioned, she bowed her head on her hand to conceal a falling tear.

At the close of the service, the Archbishop, advancing towards the Queen, addressed her thus—

"Madam, is your Majesty willing to take the oath."

The Queen replied, "I am willing."

"Will you solemnly promise and swear," continued the Archbishop, "to govern the people of this United Kingdom of Great Britain and Ireland, and the dominions thereto belonging, according to the statutes in Parliament agreed on and the respective laws and customs of the same."

"I solemnly promise so to do," said Her Majesty audibly.

"Will you to your power, cause law and justice, in mercy, to be executed in all your judgments?"

"I will."

Another long question as to whether Her Majesty would maintain the laws of God and the rights of the Church of England &c., followed, to which Her Majesty answered gently and firmly,—

"All this I promise to do."

Her Majesty, with the Lord Chamberlain and other officers, the sword of state being carried before her, then went to the altar and took the coronation oath. Laying her right hand upon the Gospels in the Bible, now brought to her by the Archbishop, she said kneeling :—

"The things which I have here before promised I will perform and keep. So help me, God!"

Then the Queen kissed the book, and set her royal sign manual to a transcript of the oath. The Duchess of Kent was observed to be visibly affected during the whole of this office.

Then, the Queen was anointed. She sat in King Edward's chair, four Knights of the Garter held a rich cloth of gold over her head, the Dean of Westminster took the ampulla from the altar, and poured some of the oil it contained into the gold anointing-spoon; then the Archbishop anointed the head and hands of the

Queen, marking them in the form of a cross and pronouncing these words—

"Be thou anointed with holy oil, as kings, priests, and prophets were anointed. And as Solomon was anointed king by Zadok the priest and Nathan the prophet, so be you anointed, blessed and consecrated Queen over this people, whom the Lord your God hath given you to rule and govern. In the name of the Father, and of the Son, and of the Holy Ghost. Amen."

The Archbishop then pronounced a prayer or blessing over the Sovereign.

The spurs were presented by the Lord Chamberlain to the Queen who returned them to the altar, and the sword of State by Viscount Melbourne, who, however, according to custom redeemed it with one hundred shillings, and carried it unsheathed before Her Majesty during the remainder of the ceremony. Then followed the investing with the Royal robe and the delivery of the orb. There was here a little confusion, and when the orb was put into the Queen's hand, she turned to Lord John Thynne, asking—

"What am I to do with it?"

"Your Majesty is to hold it if you please in your hand."

"Am I?" she said, "it is very heavy."

*As each article of the Regalia was given to the Queen the Archbishop accompanied it with suitable words. When the Queen was invested with the ring and sceptre, it was found that the ruby ring had been made for Her Majesty's little finger instead of the fourth, on which the rubric prescribed that it should be put.

"When the Archbishop was to put it on, she extended the former, but he said it must be on the latter. She replied that it was too small and that she could not get it on." As, however, the Archbishop insisted that it was right to put it there, she yielded, but had first to take off her other rings, and then this was forced on, but not without it hurting her very much, and, as soon as the ceremony was over her finger had to be bathed in iced water in order to get it off.

The Duke of Norfolk, kneeling, presented the Queen with a glove for her right hand embroidered with the arms of Howard which Her Majesty put on.

One or two more ceremonies, and then the Coronation followed. The Archbishop of Canterbury offered a prayer to God to bless Her Majesty and crown her with all princely virtues. A moment or two afterwards, the Archbishop receiving the crown from the Dean of Westminster, who took it off the altar, and accompanied by the other prelates, advanced to the Queen

---
* "The Life of Queen Victoria."

and reverently placed it upon her head. "God save the Queen" now resounded from every part of the crowded edifice, mingled with lusty cheers and accompanied by the waving of handkerchiefs. At that moment, too, Peers and Peeresses put on their coronets, the Bishops their caps, the Kings-of-arms their crowns, while trumpets sounded, drums beat, and the Park and Tower guns fired signals."

The Benediction and Te Deum having followed, the Queen was lifted or enthroned from St. Edward's chair into the chair of homage. There she sat to receive the fealty of her distinguished subjects.

The Archbishop of Canterbury knelt and did homage for himself and other Lords Spiritual, who all kissed Her Majesty's hand. The Dukes of Sussex and Cambridge, removing their coronets, each said, "I do become your liege man of life and limb and of earthly worship; and faith and truth I will bear unto you, to live and die, against all manner of folks, so help me God."

Having touched the crown on Her Majesty's head, they kissed her left cheek and then retired. The Queen's bearing towards them was very kind and affectionate. The Dukes and other Peers, then did homage, each Peer kissing the Queen's hand as he retired. Lord Rolle, who was upwards of eighty, stumbled and fell as he was going up the steps. The Queen immediately stepped forward and held out her hand to assist him amidst the loudly expressed admiration of the assembly.

Harriet Martineau wrote thus of the scene,

"The homage was as pretty a sight as any; trains of Peers touching her crown, and then kissing her hand. It was in the midst of that process that poor Lord Rolle's disaster sent a shock through the whole assemblage.......... The large infirm old man was held up by two Peers, and had nearly reached the Royal footstool when he slipped through the hands of his supporters, and rolled over and over down the steps, lying at the bottom coiled up in his robes. He was instantly lifted up, and he tried again and again, amidst shouts of admiration of his valour. The Queen at length spoke to Lord Melbourne, who stood at her shoulder, and he bowed approval, on which she rose, leaned forward, and held out her hand to the old man, dispensing with his touching the crown. He was not hurt, and his self-quizzing on his misadventure was as brave as his behaviour at the time."

Sir David Wilkie, who was present at the Coronation, wrote simply, "The Queen looked most interesting, calm and unexcited; and, as she sat upon the chair with the crown on, the sun shone from one of the windows bright upon her."

Leslie, another painter, remarked,

"I was very near the altar and the chair on which the Queen was crowned, when she signed the coronation oath I could see that she wrote a large bold hand.........I don't know why, but the first sight of her in her robes brought tears into my eyes, and it had this effect on many people: she looked almost like a child."

The ceremony of the coronation was over, and now the Archbishop of Canterbury went to the altar followed by the Queen, who gave the Lord Chamberlain her crown to hold, while she knelt before the altar.

The Gospel and Epistle of the Communion service having been read by two Bishops, Her Majesty made her offering of the chalice and patina and a purse of gold, which having been laid on the altar, she received the sacrament, kneeling on the faldstool by the chair.

Afterwards, Her Majesty put on her crown and with her sceptres in her hands took her seat again upon the throne.

The Archbishop then proceeded with the Communion Service and pronounced the final blessing. The choir sang the noble anthem "*Hallelujah! for the Lord God omnipotent reigneth.*"

The Queen then left the throne and attended by Bishops and nobles bearing the Regalia went into St. Edward's Chapel. Her Majesty delivered the sceptre with the dove to the Archbishop of Canterbury who laid it on the altar.

She was then disrobed of her imperial robe of State, and arrayed in her Royal robe of purple velvet by the Lord Chamberlain. The Archbishop placed the orb in her left hand. Her Majesty went to the west door of the Abbey wearing her crown, the sceptre with the cross being in her right, the orb in her left hand......... it was about a quarter to four o'clock when the Royal procession passed through the nave in the same order as before at the conclusion of the ceremony in the Abbey."

The Coronation had lasted more than three hours, and it must have been exceedingly fatiguing to both the body and mind of the young Queen.

As Her Majesty emerged from the western entrance of the Abbey, there came, from thousands and tens of thousands of her subjects congregated in the vicinity, thunders of acclamation and applause. Similar greetings awaited her all the way homeward, and the scene, we are told, was even more impressive than the morning, as Her Majesty now wore her crown and the Peers and Peeresses their robes and jewelled coronets. It was said that the Queen's crown had disturbed the arrangement of her soft braids of hair, and, as she returned, she was seen laughingly submitting to the help of her beautiful companion who was endeavouring to loup up the rebellious locks again.

There is one story told of this drive home which shows, as Mr. Bullock says, the self-possession and kindly consideration of the young Queen at a time of almost unexampled excitement and anxiety. Suddenly, as the Royal carriage was proceeding on its way, when they were near the Horse Guards, Her Majesty bent forward with a slightly-flushed face and half-angry expression. Calling her Master of the Horse to her she showed him some policemen who were using their truncheons to keep back the people. He at once rode off to stop them and to pass the word of command which stated that it was the Queen's special desire that all violence should be avoided.

Leslie gives us another pleasant little anecdote which shows that, notwithstanding all her honours and the great fatiguing ceremony through which Her Majesty had just been, she was, at heart, girl-like and thoroughly natural and playful. The artist tells us that she was very fond of dogs and had one favourite spaniel which was always on the look-out for her return when she had been away from home.

On that day, therefore, when Her Majesty had been absent such an unusually long time, the first sound she heard, as the State Carriage drove up to the steps of her palace, was her little favourite barking delightedly in the hall.

"There's Dash!" exclaimed the young Queen, who was instantly in a hurry to lay aside her sceptre and ball and take off her robes and crown "to go and wash little Dash."

CHAPTER VIII.

THE QUEEN'S ENGAGEMENT TO PRINCE ALBERT.

DIFFICULTIES OF THE QUEEN'S POSITION—VISIT OF THE TWO PRINCES—THE QUEEN'S PROPOSAL—LETTERS ON THE SUBJECT—HER MAJESTY'S DECLARATION TO HER PRIVY COUNCIL.

AT first when the Queen's reign began, she seems to have put aside the idea of marriage for a time, though she tells us herself that, whenever she did think of it, she never thought of being married to any one but her Cousin Prince Albert. But the correspondence between them ceased for a time, and Her Majesty's attention seemed to be more taken up with other responsibilities and duties.

There were, however, many difficulties in her position as the unmarried Queen of England. Innumerable disturbing rumours and private intrigues for the bestowal of her hand were not pleasant. And in the comparative loneliness and greatness of her lot, it was most desirable that she should have some one upon whom she could lean, to whom she could look up, and who would be united to herself in the closest of all bonds.

Her Majesty wrote herself in reference to this,

"A worse school for a young girl, or one more detrimental to all natural feelings and affections, cannot well be imagined, than the position of a Queen at eighteen, without experience and without a husband to guide and support her. This the Queen can state from painful experience, and she thanks God that none of her dear daughters are exposed to such danger."

Altogether, King Leopold had good reason for renewing his efforts to bring about the union which would, he felt sure, best secure the happiness of his niece and the welfare of a kingdom.

Therefore, he sent Prince Albert, with his brother, Prince Ernest, over to England on a visit in the Autumn of 1839. They were the bearers of a letter from the King of the Belgians to the Queen in which he recommends them as "good and honest creatures deserving your kindness, and not pedantic, but really sensible and trustworthy."

Both young men were tall and manly in figure and deportment, while, Prince Albert, we are told, was eminently handsome.

*"But there was also in his countenance a gentleness of expression, and a peculiar sweetness in his

---
* The early years of the Prince Consort.

smile, with a look of deep thought and high intelligence in his clear blue eye and expansive forehead, that added a charm to the impression he produced in those who saw him, far beyond that derived from mere regularity or beauty of features."

The Queen appears to have been still more impressed than before with Prince Albert, and in writing to her Uncle Leopold, she said, "Albert's beauty is most striking, and he is most amiable and unaffected, in short, very fascinating." Then, lest her praise of him should seem too marked, she added, "The young men are *both* amiable, and delightful companions, and I am glad to have them here."

"The way of life at Windsor during the stay of the Princes was much as follows:—the Queen breakfasting at this time in her own room, they afterwards paid her a visit there; and at two o'clock had luncheon with her and the Duchess of Kent. In the afternoon they all rode — the Queen and Duchess and the two Princes, with Lord Melbourne and most of the ladies and gentlemen in attendance forming a large cavalcade. There was a great dinner every evening, with a dance after it, three times a week."

The first incident of the visit was a little disconserting, as, the luggage of the Princes not being forthcoming, they could not appear at a Court dinner in their morning dress, but, later in the evening, they joined the circle.

Her Majesty was now pleased to show by several little marks of favour that she thought very highly of Prince Albert. She danced with him, and we are told that at one of the Castle balls, just before the Queen declared her engagement to her Council, she presented his Serene Highness with her bouquet in a most marked and significant manner. He accepted it with the fullest and most becoming sense of her kindness, but the flattering indication of her favour might have involved a less quick-witted lover in an awkward dilemma, for his uniform jacket was fastened up to the chin, after the Prussian fashion, and offered no button-hole in which to place the precious gift. But the Prince took out a pocket-knife (or was it his sword from its sheath?) and cut a slit in the breast of his coat on the left side, over the heart, where he put the flowers.

Of course there were various reports as to the way in which the decisive question was asked and answered. Her Majesty, on account of her sovereignty, was obliged to take the initiative, and to forego a girl's sweet privilege of being asked if she would bestow her hand upon her suitor.

One story runs that the Queen endeavoured to encourage her lover by asking how he liked England. To which he replied on the first day "very much," and returned the same answer the next day when the query was repeated. But on the third day, when the maiden-monarch, with downcast eyes and tell-tale blushes, asked "If he would like to live in England," he rose to the occasion. And, it is said, on this hint he spoke out those feelings which he had been treasuring in strictest secrecy.

Another story is that Her Majesty inquired of his Serene Highness whether his visit to this country had been agreeable to him?—whether he liked England? And on the answer being given, "Exceedingly," Her Majesty added, "Then it depends on you to make it your home."

All this is very pretty, but the Queen has herself told us that she directly made the proposal which she was necessitated to do from the circumstances of her case, and, afterwards, she was obliged herself to announce the fact of her engagement to her Privy Council.

Greville wrote that when the Queen "saw the Duchess of Gloucester in town, and told her she was to make her declaration the next day, the Duchess asked her if it was not a nervous thing to do.

She said, "Yes; but I did a much more nervous thing a little while ago."

"What was that?"

"I proposed to Prince Albert."

The Prince wrote about the matter as follows to his dear old Grandmother, the Dowager Duchess of Saxe-Gotha.

"The Queen sent for me alone to her room a few days ago, and declared to me in a genuine outburst of love and affection that I had gained her whole heart, and would make her intensely happy if I would make her the sacrifice of sharing my life with her, for she said she looked on it as a sacrifice; the only thing which troubled her was that she did not think she was worthy of me. The joyous openness of manner in which she told me this quite enchanted me and I was quite carried away by it."

"The Prince answered by the warmest demonstration of kindness and affection."

When the troth was plighted, the Queen adds, "I then told him to fetch Ernest, who congratulated us both and seemed very happy. He told me how perfect his brother was."

The Queen wrote to tell her friends, and, first of all, her good uncle, the King of the Belgians. To him Her Majesty said,

"My dearest Uncle,—This letter will, I am sure, give you pleasure for you have always shown and taken so warm an interest in all that concerns me. My mind is quite made up, and I told Albert this morning of it.

The warm affection he showed me on learning this gave me great pleasure. He seems perfection, and I think that I have the prospect of very great happiness before me. I love him MORE than I can say, and I shall do all in my power to render this sacrifice (for such in my opinion it is) as small as I can."

King Leopold's reply is pathetic in the depth of its gratification,

"My dearest Victoria," he said,

"Nothing could have given me greater pleasure than your dear letter. I had, when I learnt your decision, almost the feeling of Old Simeon; "Now lettest Thou. Thy servant depart in peace." Your choice has been for these last years my conviction of what might and would be best for your happiness; and just because I was convinced of it, and knew how strangely fate often changes what one tries to bring about as being the best plan one could fix upon — the maximum of a good arrangement,—I feared that it would not happen."

Prince Albert, for his part, wrote to his friend Baron Stockmar, in the following words,

"I write to you on one of the happiest days of my life, to give you the most welcome news possible," and, after having described what had taken place, he proceeded, "Victoria is so good and kind to me that I am at a loss to believe that such affection should be shown to me. I know the great interest you take in my happiness, and therefore pour out my heart to you." And he quotes,

> "Das auge sieht den Himmel offen
> Es schwimmt das Herz in seligkeit."

the passage is taken from one which has been thus rendered in English by Lord Lytton,

> "Sweet hope—and tender longing—ye
> The growth of life's first age of gold,
> When the heart, swelling, seems to see
> The gates of Heaven unfold.
> Oh, were it ever green! oh stay!
> Linger, young Love, Life's blooming May."

A happy month followed; and perhaps the very fact of the engagement having in a manner to be kept secret until Parliament had been informed of the matter added a little piquancy to the general satisfaction.

Miss Tytler writes, "On the 2nd of November there was a Review of the Batallion of the Rifle Brigade quartered at Windsor under Colonel, afterwards Sir George Brown, of Crimean fame in the Home Park. The Queen was present, accompanied by Prince Albert in the green uniform of the Coburg troops. What a picture, full of joyful content, independent of all accidents of weather, survives of the scene!

"At ten minutes to twelve I set off in my Windsor uniform and cap (already described) on my old charger 'Leopold,' with my beloved Albert looking so handsome in his uniform on my right, and Sir John Macdonald, the Adjutant-General on my left, Colonel Grey and Colonel Wemyss preceding me, a guard of honour, my other gentlemen, my cousin's gentlemen, Lady Caroline Barrington, &c., for the ground.

"A horrid day, blowing dreadfully cold, and, in addition, raining hard when we had been out a few minutes. It, however, ceased when we came to the ground. I rode alone down the ranks, and then took my place as usual, with dearest Albert on my right and Sir John Macdonald on my left, and saw the troops march past. They afterwards manœuvred. The Rifles looked beautiful. It was piercingly cold and I had my cape on, which dearest Albert settled comfortably for me. He was so cold, being *en grande tenue*, with high boots. We cantered home again, and went in to show ourselves to poor Ernest (Prince Ernest had the misfortune to suffer from jaundice), who had seen all from a window."

The Princes left Windsor on the 14th of November, and, as they visited the King of the Belgians on their way home, King Leopold could write to his niece, "I find them looking well, particularly Albert. It proves that happiness is an excellent remedy to keep people in better health than any other. He is much attached to you and modest when speaking of you. He is besides in great spirits, full of gaiety and fun."

Prince Albert wrote to his aunt and future mother-in-law,

"Dearest aunt, a thousand thanks for your two kind letters just received. I see from them that you are in close sympathy with your nephew—your son-in-law soon to be—which gratifies me very, very much......... What you say about my poor little bride sitting all alone in her room silent and sad, has touched me to the heart. Oh, that I might fly to her side to cheer her!"

To the Queen he wrote, "How often are my thoughts with you! The hours I was privileged to pass with you in your dear little room are the radiant points of my life, and I cannot even yet picture to myself that I am to be indeed so happy as to be always near you, always your protector." And he mentions touchingly and solemnly that he was going to take the Holy Sacrament in the Church at Coburg, and that, "God will not take it amiss, if in that serious act even at the altar, I think of you, for I will pray to Him for you and for your soul's health, and He will not refuse us His blessing."

The next formidable matter for the Queen to transact was to make the announcement of her engagement to her Privy Council. Surely a difficult task for the Royal Maiden.

On the 23rd eighty members of the Privy Council

assembled in the bow room on the ground floor in Buckingham Palace.

"Precisely at two," the Queen records in her journal, "I went in. The room was full, but I hardly knew who was there. Lord Melbourne I saw looking kindly at me with tears in his eyes, but he was not near me. I then read my short declaration. I felt my hands shook, but I did not make one mistake. I felt most happy and thankful when it was over. Lord Lansdowne then rose, and, in the name of the Privy Council, asked that 'this most gracious and most welcome communication might be printed.' I then left the room—the whole thing not lasting more than two or three minutes. The Duke of Cambridge came into the small library where I was standing and wished me joy."

The Queen was in the habit of wearing a bracelet containing on it the Prince's picture, and "it seemed," she added, "to give me courage at the Council."

Greville wrote of the occurrence,

"All the Privy Councillors seated themselves, when the folding doors were thrown open and the Queen came in, attired in a plain mourning-gown, but wearing a bracelet, containing Prince Albert's picture.

"She read the declaration in a clear, sonorous, sweet-toned voice, but her hands trembled so excessively that I wonder she was able to read the paper which she held."

The declaration made by the Queen is thus recorded,

"I have caused you to be summoned at the present time in order that I may acquaint you with my resolution in a matter which deeply concerns the welfare of my people, and the happiness of my future life.

"It is my intention to ally myself with the Prince Albert of Saxe-Coburg and Gotha. Deeply impressed with the solemnity of the engagement which I am about to contract, I have not come to this decision without mature consideration, nor without feeling a strong assurance that, with the blessing of Almighty God, it will at once secure my domestic felicity, and serve the interests of my country.

"I have thought fit to make this resolution known to you at the earliest period, in order that you may be apprised of a matter so highly important to me and to my kingdom, and which, I persuade myself, will be most acceptable to all my loving subjects."

"Whereupon," it is stated, "all the Privy Councillors (eighty-three members, including the Duke of Wellington, Lord Lansdowne, &c., almost all of whom are now dead) present made it their humble request to Her Majesty that Her Majesty's most gracious declaration to them might be made public; which Her Majesty was pleased to order accordingly."

The settlement of this marriage was a source of great joy, not only to the members of the Queen's

Family and especially to her mother the Duchess of Kent, who was much attached to her nephews, but, we are told, its announcement was received with great rejoicing throughout the country, and congratulations flowed in from all sides.

CHAPTER IX.

MARRIAGE OF QUEEN VICTORIA AND PRINCE ALBERT.

PRINCE ALBERT BEING INVESTED WITH THE GARTER—SORROWFUL LEAVE-TAKINGS WITH THE PRINCE'S GRANDMOTHER—A PARTING SCENE—EOS THE BEAUTIFUL GREYHOUND—ARRIVAL AT BUCKINGHAM PALACE—THE ROYAL WEDDING.

EARLY in February Lord Torrington and Colonel, (afterwards General) Grey, set out for Gotha to escort the bridegroom to England. They carried with them the Order of the Garter, which is the highest Knightly Order of England, and with which Prince Albert was invested by his father, himself a Knight, before the whole Court of Gotha.

One hundred and one guns were fired to commemorate the auspicious occasion. The tutor under whom Prince Albert had studied at Bonn wrote of the event, "The Grand-Ducal Papa bound the Garter round his boy's knee amidst the roar of a hundred and one cannon. (The attaching of the order, however, was not done by Prince Albert's father but by the Prince of Leiningen, the Queen's half-brother, another Knight of the Order.) The earnestness and gravity with which the Prince has obeyed this early call to take a European position, give him dignity and standing in spite of his youth and increase the charm of his whole aspect."

The investiture was followed by a grand dinner, when the Queen's health was drunk by a large company, standing, the band playing "God save the Queen," meanwhile, trumpets blowing and the artillery outside firing a royal salute.

Then came some sorrowful leave-takings which must have been deeply felt by one who had such tender and strong affections as Prince Albert.

The Prince with his thoughtful, pensive temperament, had in the very beginning of his engagement, foreseen that there would be a dark side to the cloud whose silver lining seemed just then so radiantly bright.

He had written to his step-mother,—

"With the exception of my relations towards her (the Queen) my future position will have its dark sides, and the sky will not always be blue and unclouded. But life has its thorns in every position, and the consciousness of having used one's powers and endeavours for an object so great as that of promoting the good of so many, will surely be sufficient to support me."

And again to a college friend,—

"My future lot is high and brilliant but also plentifully strewed with thorns.........The separation from my native country—from dear Coburg—from so many friends is very painful to me!"

The leave-taking with his grandmother, the Dowager Duchess of Gotha, who had partly brought him up, was terribly trying. The old lady felt that the coming separation with her beloved grandson, if not absolutely final, must be complete and lasting; and what consideration of earthly grandeur or high position could reconcile her to the thought; yet, though her grief was great, we are told that she received the English gentlemen who had come to escort her grandson to his new home, and was much affected by their visit. "She was very deaf," General Grey writes, "but it was really painful to witness her efforts to keep down her grief. She took the gentlemen over her rooms, showed them her pictures, &c, but the conversation always came back to Prince Albert, and his name was never mentioned without a fresh burst of tears!"

Again, General Grey wrote, "The departure from Gotha was an affecting scene, and everything showed the genuine love of all classes for their young Prince. The streets were densely crowded; every window was crammed with heads; every house-top covered with people waving handkerchiefs, and vying with each other in demonstrations of affection that could not be mistaken. The carriages stopped in passing the Dowager Duchess's, and Prince Albert got out, with his father and brother, to bid her a last adieu. It was a terrible trial to the poor Duchess, who was inconsolable for the loss of her beloved grandson. She came to the window as the carriage drove off, and threw her arms out, calling out, "Albert, Albert," in tones that went to everyone's heart, when she was carried away, almost in a fainting state by her attendants!"

At one place, where M. Stein the minister, and others who had preceded the Royal party so far, took their leave, and where the Duke (who, with Prince Ernest, was accompanying Prince Albert to England) got into his travelling-carriage and the journey to England was fairly begun, an arch of green fir-trees had been erected, and a number of young girls dressed in white, with roses and garlands, and a band of musicians, were assembled to bid a final "God speed" to the young Prince who was leaving his native land behind him. It was a pretty sight but bitterly cold. The ground covered with snow, a hard frost, and a bitter northeast wind were scarcely in keeping with white muslin gowns and wreaths of flowers.

It is needless to say that, in spite of the vexed questions which the matter of his income and of his future precedence as the husband of our Queen had been in Parliament, the Prince's receptions at Dover and at Canterbury were most enthusiastic. And even the unfortunate nature of the weather, for it poured with rain, did not prevent immense crowds from assembling at Dover to see the Prince depart, or from turning out in every village through which he passed on his way to Canterbury to welcome him with hearty English cheers. His reception at Canterbury was everything that could be desired. The Royal party arrived at two and were welcomed by the multitudes which thronged the streets. Having received an address from the City authorities, the Prince, with his brother, attended the service of the Cathedral at three. The City was illuminated in the evening, and, vast crowds having assembled before the hotel, they cheered and called for the Prince, who appeared, to their great delight, on the balcony.

It had been arranged that his Serene Highness should not arrive at Buckingham Palace till Saturday the 8th, but the Prince sent on his valet from Canterbury with his favourite greyhound "Eôs," and the Queen mentions in her Journal how pleased she was to see "dear Eôs" the evening before the arrival of the Prince.

The beautiful animal had been over to England before with the Prince in 1839. Its Royal master had brought it up himself and trained it from the time it was six weeks old. It was jet black, with the exception of a narrow white streak on the nose, and a white foot; and it was most sagacious and much attached to its master. It died at Windsor about four years after the marriage of the Queen and Prince, and a bronze model of it now marks the spot where it was buried.

On Saturday morning, after receiving an address from the Dean and ·Chapter, the Prince left at ten for London, meeting with the same enthusiastic reception everywhere, until he arrived at Buckingham Palace, at half-past four, where the Queen herself, with her mother, and attended by the whole household, received him at the hall-door.

The Queen recorded in her journal the great joy she felt at seeing the Prince again. He brought her as his wedding gift a beautiful diamond and sapphire brooch, and she gave him, in return, the star and badge of the Garter, and the Garter itself set in diamonds.

A great dinner was given that evening after the Lord Chancellor had administered the oaths of naturalisation to the Prince, and the following day, after the Queen and Prince had attended Divine service, the latter paid formal visits to the members of the Royal Family. Again there was a great dinner in the evening, and then the wedding day Monday the 10th of February dawned.

But in all the excitement and splendour of that day

the Prince did not forget his dear old grandmother. On the morning of the wedding-day he sent her these few touching lines,

"Dear Grandmamma,

"In less than three hours I shall stand before the altar with my dear bride! In these solemn moments I must once more ask your blessing, which I am well assured I shall receive, and which will be my safeguard and my future joy! I must end. God help me. Ever your faithful Grandson."

The thoughtful Prince could not ignore, even in the near prospect of so much happiness with his wife, the fact that, as a stranger in the land, he would have much to live down and would have in a measure to make his own position among the English people.

We are told an interesting story of the Queen and her approaching marriage. It is said the Archbishop of Canterbury waited upon Her Majesty, and enquired if it were her wish that any alteration should be made in that portion of the wedding service which included a promise of obedience—such a promise being a curious one for the Queen of Great Britain to make to her newly naturalized subject who had just taken the oath to her as his liege lady. The Queen, according to the report, replied that, "it was her wish to be married in all respects like any other woman, according to the revered usages of the Church of England, and that, though not as a *Queen*, as a *woman* she was ready to promise all things contained in that portion of the Liturgy.

The wedding-morning was cold, foggy and wet, yet, notwithstanding that, vast crowds assembled in St. James's Park and its approaches, and even the inclement weather could not damp the joy of the Queen's subjects. More than a century had elapsed since the nuptials of a reigning Queen of England had been celebrated, besides which, the youth and grace of Victoria appealed strongly to the hearts of the people. Many a fervent "God bless her," was uttered by the citizens of London as they thought of the Royal bride.

The *Times* described the mass of spectators wedged in at the back of Carlton Terrace and the foot of Constitution Hill, and the immense quantity of chairs, tables, benches, even casks pressed into the service and affording vantage-ground to those who could pay for the accommodation. "The dripping trees were also rendered available and had their branches so laden with human fruit, that brittle boughs gave way, while single specimens and small clusters of men and boys came rattling down on the heads of confiding fellow-creatures; but such misadventures were without serious accident, and simply afforded additional entertainment to the self-invited, light-hearted wedding-guests."

At a quarter before twelve the bridegroom's procession issued forth, consisting of Prince Albert, his father, the Duke of Saxe-Coburg-Gotha, his brother Prince Ernest and their suites.

Prince Albert was received with eager clappings of hands and waving of handkerchiefs. He was dressed in the uniform of a British Field-Marshal and wore only one decoration, that of the Garter, with the collar surmounted by two white rosettes, and his bride's gifts of the previous day, the George and Star set in diamonds, on his breast, and the diamond-embroidered Garter round his knee. "His pale handsome face, with its slight brown moustache, his slender yet manly figure would have become any dress. Indeed his general appearance, 'full of thoughtful grace and quiet dignity' impressed every honest observer most favourably."

His father and brother, hitherto his dearest friends, walked by his side. The Duke of Saxe-Coburg and Gotha, it is said, must have looked like one of the quaint stately figures out of an old German print, in his long military boots and his dark green uniform turned up with red. He, also, wore the collar and star of the Garter, and the star of his own Order of Coburg-Gotha. Prince Ernest, on the contrary, was in a gay light blue and silver uniform, and carried his helmet in his hand. He was a fine young man, whose face it was thought looked a little stern in its repressed emotion.

At ten minutes past twelve the signal was given for the departure of the Queen. The Duchess of Kent, and the Duchess of Sutherland drove in the State carriage with Her Majesty "at a slow pace," for the Royal Bride, even on her bridal day did not forget the claim of her subjects upon her. A strong escort of Household cavalry prevented the pressure of the shouting crowds from being overpowering.

The Queen wore a bride's dress of white satin and orange blossoms, a simple wreath of orange-blossoms on her fair hair. Her magnificent veil of Honiton lace did not cover the fair face, but fell on either side of the bent head. Her ornaments were the brooch which had been the bridegroom's gift, diamond earrings and necklace, and the collar and insignia of the Garter. We are told she was a true woman then, and looked well in her natural agitation. "She was shy and a little shrinking," Miss Tytler says, "as became a bride and her eyes were swollen with recent tears—an illustration of the wise old Scotch proverb, 'A greetin' (weeping) bride's a happy bride.'"

The Duchess, too, whose motherly heart shared faithfully in her daughter's perturbation, looked "disconsolate," and it must have been a trying ordeal for her, who was thus resigning the first place in that daughter's heart for whom she had sacrificed and done so very much.

The wedding was celebrated with all due magnificence in the Chapel Royal, St. James's. The altar was splendidly decorated and laden with gold plate. Four state seats were set—one for the Queen, one for Prince Albert, one for the Queen-Dowager and one for the Duchess of Kent. A host of celebrities and of young and fashionable women had assembled in the Chapel as early as ten o'clock.

At twenty minutes past twelve, the bridegroom walked up the aisle, carrying a prayer book covered with green velvet. He advanced bowing to each side, followed by his supporters to the altar-rail, before which were the four chairs of state.

The Queen entered the chapel at twenty-five minutes to one, and immediately proceeding to her chair, knelt and prayed and then seated herself. Her mother was on her left side. Behind her stood her bridesmaids and train-bearers, twelve unmarried ladies, who were dressed like the Queen, except that they wore no veils and wore white roses instead of orange blossoms. The loveliness of this group of noble ladies attracted universal admiration.

The Archbishop of Canterbury and the Bishop of London were already at the Altar, and in a few moments the Queen and the Prince advanced to the Communion table.

THE ROYAL FAMILY.

The service was the beautiful simple marriage service of the Church of England unchanged in any respect.

In reply to the question, "Who giveth this woman to be married to this man?" the Duke of Sussex presented himself.

The Prince and the Queen's Christian names, Albert and Victoria were all the names used. Prince Albert answered firmly to the usual questions, "I will."

The corresponding inquiries were then addressed to Her Majesty,—

"Victoria, wilt thou have Albert to thy wedded husband, to live together after God's ordinance in the holy estate of matrimony? Wilt thou obey him and serve him, love, honour and keep him in sickness and in health, and, forsaking all other, keep thee only unto him, so long as ye both shall live?"

The Queen replied, we are told, in accents which, though full of softness and music, were audible at the most extreme corner of the chapel, "I will," and in so responding, she accompanied the expression with a glance at His Royal Highness which convinced all who beheld it that her heart was with her words.

When the Archbishop asked,—

"Who giveth this woman to be married to this man?" the Duke of Sussex advanced, and, holding the Queen's hand, said, "I do."

The Archbishop then took Her Majesty's hand, and

placed it in that of Prince Albert whereupon the usual trothing forms were gone through. One who was present at the ceremony observed that the Queen's utterance of the words "love cherish and obey," and the confiding look with which they were accompanied was very beautiful.

Prince Albert next took the wedding-ring, which was quite plain, off his own finger and gave it to the Archbishop. His Grace handed it back to the Prince who then placed it, as directed, on his wife's finger.

At that moment, the Earl of Uxbridge gave the signal and the cannon fired the Royal Salute which was answered by the Tower artillery and the Park guns firing, while all the bells in London and Westminster rang out a joyous peal, upon which it became known far and wide that our Queen had become a married woman.

The remaining portions of the Service having been read by the Archbishop, and the benediction having been pronounced, the Queen shook hands cordially with the several members of the Royal Family. The Duke of Sussex having shaken hands warmly with the Royal Bride affectionately kissed her cheek.

The procession having been formed, left the chapel in much the same order as it had entered. But the Queen and her husband now walked together hand in hand, ungloved—Prince Albert with sparkling eyes and

THE ROYAL FAMILY. 119

a heightened colour smiling down upon the Queen while she appeared very bright and animated.

When the Queen and Prince passed through the corridor, after leaving the chapel, the clapping of hands and waving of handkerchiefs were renewed and continued until they had vanished out of sight. Prince Albert it is said, held Her Majesty's hand in his in such a way as to display the wedding-ring, which appeared to be a very solid one.

The Queen, Prince Albert, their Royal relatives and the Principal Ministers of State and Members of the Privy Council now left the procession and proceeded to the throne-room. The Royal Bride and Bridegroom here signed the marriage register. The marriage was attested by the Duke of Sussex and twenty-nine other persons. Among the witnesses who signed was the Duke of Wellington, whose signature had also appeared at the attestation of Her Majesty's birth. The attestation book which is bound in rich purple velvet, is a speaking memento of Royal nuptials ceremonies for many generations past. It is in the custody of the Archbishop of Canterbury.

On the return journey, Prince Albert drove in the same carriage with the Queen. Her Majesty sat in the place of honour and her husband and mother sat opposite.

The people were so wishful to see the Queen and

were so eager in their demonstrations of loyalty, that she put down the closed windows of her carriage and smiled and bowed most graciously to her loyal subjects.

The Dowager Lady Lyttleton, an eye-witness of the scene, has thus written about the chief actor in it,—

"The Queen's look and manner were very pleasing, her eyes much swollen with tears, but great happiness in her countenance, and her look of confidence and comfort at the Prince when they walked away together as man and wife was very pleasing to see. I understand she is in extremely high spirits since; such a new thing for her to *dare* to be unguarded in conversation with any body, and, with her frank and fearless nature, the restraints she has hitherto been under from one reason or another with everybody must have been most painful."

The wedding breakfast was given at Buckingham Palace. The Archbishop of Canterbury, the Bishop of London, the various members of the Royal Family, the Ministers of State and the officers of the household were included among the guests.

The wedding cake, admirably designed, was an object of great attraction. More than nine feet in circumference, by sixteen inches deep, its weight was three hundred pounds, and the materials of which it was composed cost one hundred guineas. On the top of the cake was the figure of Britannia in the act of blessing the illustrious Bride and Bridegroom. The figures were nearly a foot in height and by the feet of the Prince was the effigy of a dog, intended to represent fidelity, while at the feet of the Queen were two turtle-doves denoting happiness. The whole thing was artistically and beautifully decorated.

Shortly before four o'clock the Royal party left Buckingham Palace for Windsor amid the acclamations of a vast multitude. The weather had changed, and just as the Royal Procession left the palace the sun shone forth brilliantly upon the newly-married pair, an emblem, it was hoped, of their future happiness.

Her Majesty's travelling-dress was a pelisse of white satin trimmed with swansdown, a white satin bonnet, and feather. The Prince was in a plain dark travelling-dress.

Thus, our Queen and the Prince Consort were married and the occasion gave cause for the following lines from the pen of Elizabeth Barret Browning,—

> "She vows to love, who vowed to rule, the chosen at her side,
> Let none say, 'God preserve the Queen,' but rather 'Bless the Bride,'
> None blow the trump, none bend the knee, none violate the dream
> Wherein no monarch but a wife, she to herself may seem;
> Or if you say, 'Preserve the Queen,' oh, breathe it inward, low—
> She is a *woman* and *beloved*, and 'tis enough but so.

Count it enough, thou noble Prince, who tak'st her by the hand,
And claimest for thy lady-love our Lady of the land.
And since, Prince Albert, men have called thy spirit high and rare,
And true to truth and brave to truth as some at Augsburg were,
We charge thee by thy loyal thoughts and by thy poet mind,
Which not by glory and degree takes measure of mankind,
Esteem that wedded hand less dear for sceptre than for ring,
And hold her uncrowned womanhood to be the Royal thing."

CHAPTER X.

EARLY MARRIED LIFE..

PRINCE ALBERT'S PARTING WITH HIS FATHER—WRITING TO HIS GRANDMOTHER—EASTER COMMUNION WITH THE QUEEN—A SERIOUS ACCIDENT—PARTING WITH PRINCE ERNEST—SKETCH OF THE DAILY LIFE OF THE PRINCE AND QUEEN—THEIR INTEREST IN ART—MENDELSSOHN'S REMINISCENCES.

THE Queen was now married to the husband of her choice, amid the sincere and general rejoicings of her subjects; "It is that," Lord Melbourne said to the Queen, "which makes your Majesty's marriage so popular, as they know it is not for mere State reasons."

And from the glimpses which have been revealed to us, we judge the married life of the Royal Pair was, from its very commencement, a singularly unique and happy one. It is true there were shadows, some of which Prince Albert had wisely and thoughtfully foreseen, but there was also much real happiness.

About a fortnight after the marriage, Prince Albert had to part with his father, the Duke of Coburg, who left England on the 28th. This separation the Prince felt very deeply.

"He said to me," the Queen records in her Journal, "that I had never known a father, and could not therefore feel what he did. His childhood had been very happy."

"Ernest (Prince Ernest remained for some time longer in England), he said, was now the only one remaining here of all his earliest ties and recollections; but that if I continued to love him as I did now I could make up for it all. He never cried, he said, in general, but Alvensleben and Kolowraith" (who had accompanied the Duke to England and had now returned with him), "had cried so much that he was quite overcome. Oh, how I did feel for my dearest, precious husband at this moment! Father, brother, friends, country—all has he left, and all for me."

Levees, Drawing-rooms, Presentations, Addresses, great-dinners, State visits to the theatres, &c., followed the marriage in rapid succession. And, at first, the change in his mode of life and the late hours were very trying to the Prince.

Writing to his grandmother on the 24th, he says, "Victoria and I are quite well. We are very happy and in good spirits, but I find it very difficult to acclimatise myself completely, though I hope soon to find myself more at home. The late hours are what I find it most difficult to bear."

Easter was spent at Windsor, when the Queen and Prince took the Holy Sacrament together for the first time in St. George's Chapel.

Her Majesty says in a Memorandum,—

"The Prince had a very strong feeling about the solemnity of this act, and did not like to appear in company either the evening before, or on the day on which he took it, and he and the Queen almost always dined alone on these occasions."

On another occasion, a few months later, Her Majesty says,—

"We two dined together, as Albert likes being quite alone before he takes the Sacrament, we played part of Mozart's Requiem, and then he read to me out of the "Stunden der Andacht (Hours of Devotion) the article on Self-knowledge."

On Easter Monday, April 20th, the Prince met with a serious, and what might have been a fatal accident, which occurred before the Queen's very eyes. The stag-hounds were to meet at Ascot, and it had been arranged that the Prince should go out with them and that the Queen should follow to the Heath later with his brother Prince Ernest.

Before he set out the Prince Albert happened to say lightly to the Queen,—

"I hope we shall meet again."

On leaving the Castle, attended by some few gentlemen, His Royal Highness, who was mounted on a handsome but very vicious thorough-bred horse called "Tom Bowling," cantered past the window at which the Queen was standing. Taking the bit between his teeth, the horse suddenly ran away at the top of his speed, and the Prince, after turning him several times, was at last knocked off by a tree, against which he brushed in passing, and fell, happily and most providentially, considering the pace at which he was going, without being seriously hurt.

The Queen relates in her Journal, describing what she saw,—

"Albert's horse seemed to go very fast and jumped very much. He turned him round several times, and then I saw him run away violently through the trees and disappear. I ran anxiously to Albert's room in hopes of seeing something, but could not. Mr. Cowper rode back, and I heard him say Albert was not hurt. Almost immediately afterwards I saw dearest Albert ride out of the gate. I sent for Ernest and he told me Albert had had a fall, but was not hurt!"

When the Queen arrived at Ascot, her Journal continues, "Albert received me on the terrace of the large stand, and led me up. He looked very pale and said he had been much alarmed lest I should have been frightened by his accident...... He told me he scraped the skin off his poor arm, had bruised his hip and knee, and his coat was torn and dirty. It was a frightful fall, and might (I shudder to think of the danger my dearest, precious inestimable husband was in) have been nearly fatal.

The horse ran away from the *very* door, Albert said. He turned him round and round, lost his stirrup, and then he dashed through the trees, and threw Albert violently against a tree, the last near the wall, the force of which brought him to the ground......... Oh, how thankful I am that it was no worse! His anxiety was all for me and not for himself."

This scene speaks for itself of the utter devotion of each to each, and of the complete happiness of the married life thus tragically threatened in its commencement.

On the 9th of May, Prince Albert's brother, Ernest, the Hereditary Prince, left England, and his departure was a great grief to Prince Albert.

The Queen relates that, according to a custom among German students, the two brothers sang a very pretty song together called "*Abschied*," (Farewell.) Prince Albert was much affected, and, when the Queen ran upstairs, she found him looking, "pale as a sheet and his eyes full of tears."

"After a little while," Her Majesty adds, "he said, 'Such things are hard to bear,' which indeed they are."

In the "Early Years of the Prince Consort," the daily life of the Royal couple in their early married life is thus described, by Her Majesty,

"At this time the Prince and Queen seem to have spent their day much as follows: They breakfasted at nine, and took a walk every morning soon afterwards. Then came the usual amount of business (far less heavy, however, than now) besides which they drew and etched a great deal together, which was a source of great amusement, having the plates 'bit' in the house. Luncheon followed at the usual hour of two o'clock. Lord Melbourne, who was generally staying in the house, came to the Queen in the afternoon, and between five and six the Prince usually drove her out in a pony phaeton. If the Prince did not drive the Queen, he rode, in which case she took a drive with the Duchess of Kent or the ladies. The Prince also read aloud most days to the Queen. The dinner was at eight o'clock, and always with the company. In the evening the Prince frequently played at double chess, a game of which he was very fond, and which he played extremely well.

The Prince was also, at this time, much occupied with painting of which he was very fond but for which, in after years, he had no time.

He "began a picture of the death of Posa from Schiller's *Don Carlos*, making first a small sketch for it, which he did beautifully."

The fine tastes of the Prince for music and drawing, which the Queen could so thoroughly appreciate and enter into, must have given them both much real and healthy enjoyment.

We have an interesting glimpse of the Royal pair given us by Uwins, in a letter dated August 15th 1843, which, Sir Theodore Martin says, "is valuable as showing the impression produced by their visits upon one of not the least gifted of the artists in whose labours they testified so warm an interest." These were artists who were engaged in decorating a summer-house or Pavilion in the garden of Buckingham Palace with frescopainting. The Queen and Prince watched their progress with great interest, the Prince being a great admirer of the art and having thrown himself with great zeal into the question of its applicability for the decoration of the houses of Parliament.

Mr. Uwin writes,

"The opportunity so lately afforded me of becoming acquainted with the habits, tastes, and in some degree with the intellectual acquirements of the Prince and the Queen has greatly increased my respect for them.

"History, literature, science and art seem to have lent their stores to form the mind of the Prince. He is really an accomplished man, and withal possesses so much good sense and consideration, that, taken apart from his playfulness and good humour, he might pass for an aged and experienced person, instead of a youth of two or three and twenty.

"The Queen, too, is full of intelligence, her observations very acute, and her judgment apparently matured beyond her age.

"It has happened to me in life to see something of many Royal personages, and I must say, with the single exception of the Duke of Kent, I have never met with any either in England or on the Continent of Europe, who have impressed me so favourably as our reigning Sovereign, and her young and interesting husband.

"Coming to us twice a day unannounced and without attendants, entirely stript of all state and ceremony, courting conversation, and desiring rather reason than obedience, they have gained our admiration and love.

"In many things they are an example to the age. They have breakfasted (they had now got into the way of having earlier hours), heard morning prayers with the household in the private Chapel, and are out some distance from the Palace talking to us in the Summerhouse, before half-past nine o'clock—sometimes earlier. After the public duties of the day and before their dinner, they come out again, evidently delighted to get away from the bustle of the world to enjoy each other's society in the solitude of the garden.

"Our peaceful pursuits are in accordance with the scene........."

As regards music, too, Prince Albert early revealed his predilection towards it. His first appearance in connection with music, we are told, was at the Ancient Music Concerts.

But in private he played and sang much with the Queen, his favourite instrument being the organ.

Lady Lyttleton thus relates her impression of one musical evening:

"Yesterday evening, as I was sitting here comfortably after the drive, by candle-light, reading M. Guizot, there suddenly arose from the room beneath—oh, such sounds! It was Prince Albert, dear Prince Albert, playing on the organ, and with such master skill, as it appeared to me—modulating so learnedly, winding through every kind of bass and chord, till he wound up with the most perfect cadence; and then off again, louder, and then softer; no tune, as I was too distant to perceive the execution or small touches, so I only heard the harmony; but I never listened with much more pleasure to any music. I ventured at dinner to ask him what I had heard.

Oh! my organ—a new possession of mine. I am so fond of the organ! It is the first of instruments;

the only instrument for expressing one's feelings. (I thought, are they not good feelings that the organ expresses?) and it teaches to play; for on the organ a mistake, oh! such misery;' and he quite shudd-red at the thought of the discord."

A most interesting and graphic account of a visit to the Queen and Prince Albert by Mendelssohn in the Summer of 1842, is given to us in a letter to his mother,

"I must tell you," writes the great Musician "all the details of my last visit to Buckingham Palace. It is, as G. says, the one really pleasant and thoroughly comfortable English house where one feels *à son aise.* Of course, I do know a few others; but yet on the whole I agree with him. Joking apart, Prince Albert had asked me to go to him on Saturday at two o'clock, so that I might try his organ before I left England. I found him alone, and as we were walking away the Queen came in, also alone, in a simple morning dress. She said she was obliged to leave for Claremont in an hour: and then suddenly interrupting herself, exclaimed, 'But, goodness! what a confusion!' For the wind had littered- the whole room, and even the pedals of the organ (which, by the way, made a very pretty feature in the room) with leaves of music from a large portfolio that lay open. As she spoke she knelt down and began picking up the music. Prince Albert helped, and I, too, was not idle. Then Prince Albert proceeded to explain the stops to me, and she said that she would meanwhile put things straight.

"I begged that the Prince would first play me something, so that, as I said, I might boast about it in Germany; and he played a chorale by heart, with the pedals, so charmingly and clearly and correctly, that it would have done credit to any professional; and the Queen, having finished her work, came and sat by him, and listened and looked pleased.

"Then it was my turn, and I began my chorus from *St. Paul,*—

'*How lovely are the Messengers.*'

Before I got to the end of the first verse, they both joined in the chorus; and all the time Prince Albert managed the stops for me so cleverly—first a flute, at the *forte* the great organ, at the D major part of the whole; then he made a lovely *diminuendo* with the stops, and so on to the end of the piece, and all by heart, that I was really quite enchanted.

Then the young Prince of Gotha came in, and there was more chatting; and the Queen asked if I had written any new songs, and said she was very fond of singing my published ones.

'You should sing one to him,' said Prince Albert; and after a little begging, she said she would try the *Fruhlingslied* (Song of the Spring) in B flat—'If it is still here,' she added, 'for all my music is packed up for Claremont.'

"Prince Albert went to look for it, but came back saying it was already packed.

'But one might perhaps unpack it,' said I.

'We must send for Lady ——,' she said, (I did not catch the name.) So the bell was rung and the servants were sent after it, but without success; and at last the Queen went herself, and while she was gone, Prince Albert said to me,—

"'She begs you will accept this present as a remembrance,' and gave me a little case with a beautiful ring, on which is engraved—'*V. R.* 1842.'

"Then the Queen came back and said:—

"'Lady —— is gone, and has taken all my things with her. It really is most annoying.' (You can't think how that amused me.) I then begged that I might not be made to suffer for the accident, and hoped she would sing another song. After some consultation with her husband, he said, 'She will sing you something of Glück's.'

"Meanwhile, the Princess of Gotha had come in; and we five proceeded through various corridors and rooms to the Queen's sitting-room, where there was a gigantic rocking-horse standing near the sofa, and two big bird-cages, and pictures on the walls, and bound books on the table—music on the piano.

THE ROYAL FAMILY.

"The Duchess of Kent came in too; and while they were all talking I rummaged about amongst the music, and soon discovered my first set of songs.

"So, of course, I begged her rather to sing one of those than the Glück, to which she very kindly consented; and which did she choose?—'*Schöner und Schöner Schmückt sich!*'—sang it quite charmingly, in strict time and tune, and with very good execution. Only in the line '*Der Prosa Lasten und Müh*,' where it goes down to D, and comes up again chromatically, she sang D sharp each time; and as I gave her the note both times, the last time she sang D, and there it ought to have been D sharp. But with the exception of this little mistake, it was really charming, and the last long G I have never heard better or purer or more natural from any amateur. Then I was obliged to confess that Fanny had written the song (which I found very hard, but pride must have a fall) and begged her to sing one of my own also. If I would give her plenty of help she would gladly try, she said; and then she sang the Pilgerspruch (Pilgrim's Speech) "*Lass dich nur*," really quite faultlessly, and with charming feeling and expression.

"I thought to myself one must not pay too many compliments on such an occasion; so I merely thanked her a great many times, upon which she said:—

"Oh, if only I had not been so frightened: generally I have such long breath."

"Then I praised her heartily, and with the best conscience in the world; for just that part with the long C at the close she had done so well, taking the three following and connecting notes in the same breath, as one seldom hears it done; and therefore it amused me doubly that she herself should have begun about it.

"After this Prince Albert sang the *Arndte-lied*, "*Es ist ein Schnitter;*" and then he said I must play him something before I went, and gave me as themes the chorale which he had played on the organ and the song he had just sung. If everything had gone as usual I ought to have improvised most dreadfully badly —for it is almost always like that with me when I want it to go well—and then I should have gone away vexed the whole morning.

"But—just as if I was to keep nothing but the pleasantest, most charming recollection of it—I never improvised better. I was in the best mood for it, and played a long time, and enjoyed it myself; so that between the two themes I brought in the songs that the Queen had sung, naturally enough; and it all went off so easily that I would gladly not have stopped; and they followed me with so much intelligence and attention that I felt more at ease than I ever did in improvising to an audience. She said several times she hoped I would soon come to England again and pay them a visit; and then I took leave.

"And down below I saw the beautiful carriages waiting, with their scarlet out-riders; and in a quarter of an hour the flag was lowered, and the *Court Circular* announced: "Her Majesty left the Palace at twenty minutes past three.".........

"I must add that I begged the Queen to allow me to dedicate my A minor Symphony to her, as that had really been the inducement to my journey, and because the English name on the Scotch piece would look doubly well. Also, I forgot to tell you how, just as she was going to begin to sing, she said,

"But the parrot must go out first, or he will screech louder than I shall sing."

"Upon which Prince Albert rang the bell; and the Prince of Gotha said he would carry it out; and I said 'Allow me,' and I carried the great cage out, to the astonishment of the servants."

Such an insight into the domestic life of the Queen and Prince, and such praise of Her Majesty's and the Prince's talents from so great an authority is deeply interesting.

CHAPTER XI.

THE YOUNG ROYAL PARENTS.

MORE ABOUT PRINCE ALBERT—HIS AND THE QUEEN'S LOVE OF THE COUNTRY—BIRTH OF THE PRINCESS ROYAL—BIRTH OF THE PRINCE OF WALES—CHRISTMAS-TREES.—THE TITLES OF THE INFANT PRINCE.

PRINCE ALBERT proposed for himself a wise and generous course, which he embodied in these words,—

"To sink his own individual existence in that of his wife, to aim at no power by himself or for himself, to shun all ostentation, to assume no separate responsibilities before the public; continually and anxiously to watch every part of the public business in order to be able to advise and assist her at any moment, in any of the multifarious and difficult questions brought before her—sometimes political, or social, or personal—as the natural head of the family, superintendent of her household, manager of her private affairs, her sole confidential adviser in politics and only assistant in her communications with the affairs of the Government."

He expressed his object very modestly in writing to his father by saying,

"I endeavour quietly to be of as much use to Victoria as I can."

The post which the Prince thus occupied was one beset with difficulties; which would have been even greater if it had not been for the perfect confidence which existed between the Queen and himself, and his perfect self-command, which enabled him always to be forbearing and courteous to others under every provocation.

Attempts were made to keep the Prince from occupying his proper place and to make him feel that he was only the husband and not the master of the house, but the Queen entirely disapproved of this, for she was too true a woman to forget that she had vowed at the altar not only to love and cherish but also to obey. She looked upon that marriage vow as a "sacred obligation which she could consent neither to limit nor refine away."

We are told in "*Early Years of the Prince Consort,*" by General Grey that, "From the moment of his establishment in the English Palace as the husband of the Queen, his first object was to maintain, and if possible even raise the character of the Court. With this view he knew that it was not enough that his own conduct should be, in truth, free from reproach, no shadow of a shade of suspicion should, by possibility, attach to it. He knew that, in his position, every action would be scanned—not always, possibly, in a friendly spirit; that his goings out and comings in would be watched, and that in every society, however little disposed to be censorious, there would always be found some prone, where an opportunity afforded, to exaggerate, and even invent stories against him, and to put an uncharitable construction on the most innocent acts.

"He therefore, from the first, laid down strict, not to say severe rules, for his own guidance. He imposed a degree of restraint and self-denial upon his own movements, which could not but have been irksome, had he not been sustained by a sense of the advantage which the throne would derive from it. He denied himself the pleasure—which, to one so fond as he was of personally watching and inspecting every movement that was in progress, would have been very great—of walking at will about the town. Wherever he went, whether in a carriage or on horseback, he was accompanied by his equerry. He paid no visits in general society. His visits were to the studio of the artist, to museums of art or science, to institutions for good and benevolent purposes. Wherever a visit from him, or his presence could tend to advance the real good of his people, there his horses might be seen waiting; never at the door of mere fashion. Scandal itself could take no liberty with his name. He loved to ride through all the districts of London where building and improvements were in progress, more especially when they were such as would conduce to the health or recreation of the working classes; and few, if any took such interest as he did in all that was being done, at any distance, east, west, north or south of the great city—from Victoria Park to Battersea—from the Regents Park to the Crystal Palace and far beyond.

'He would frequently return,' Her Majesty says, 'to luncheon, at a great pace,' and would always come through the Queen's dressing-room, where she generally was at that time, with that bright, loving smile with which he ever greeted her; telling her where he had been—what new buildings he had seen—what studios, &c., he had visited.

Riding for riding's sake he disliked, and said :—

'Es ennuyirt mich so, (It bores me so.)'

"Albert the Good" plainly believed as his daughter, Princess Alice, wrote long afterwards, that life is made for work and not for pleasure.

But he was fully capable of enjoying to the full all that could please a most refined and cultured taste.

He was ever exceedingly fond of the country and delighted in the beauties of nature. We are told that before his marriage when he was staying at Florence it was his great delight to take long walks in the beautiful country around. And then he would become at once gay and animated, saying, "Now I can breathe —now I am happy!"

In "Early years," the Queen says in a note, when this characteristic had been mentioned,

"This the Prince constantly expressed on arriving at Osborne and Balmoral, and on leaving London. 'How sweets it smells! How delicious the air is! One begins to breathe again!' And how he delighted in the songs of birds and especially of nightingales!—listening for them in the happy peaceful walks he used to take with the Queen in the woods at Osborne, and whistling to them in their own peculiar long note, which they invariably answer! The Queen cannot hear this note now without fancying she hears him, and without the deepest, saddest emotion. At night he would stand on the balcony, at Osborne, in May, listening to the nightingales."

The Queen's love for the country seems to have grown much stronger after her union with Prince Albert. She records in her Journal,—

"I told Albert that formerly I was too happy to go to London and wretched to leave it, and how, since the blessed hour of my marriage, and still more since the summer, I dislike and am unhappy to leave the country and could be content and happy never to go to town. This pleased him. The solid pleasures of a peaceful, quiet, yet happy life in the country, with my inestimable husband and friend, my all in all, are far more durable than the amusements of London, though we don't despise or dislike these sometimes."

As years went by this preference of the Queen fo the country increased, and her two books "Leaves from the Journal of Our Life in the Highland," and "More Leaves from the Queen's Journal," testify to the pleasure with which Her Majesty found herself, "far from the madding crowd," in comparative seclusion and rural quiet.

When the little Princess Royal was born there were great rejoicings. The Prince wrote to his father, "The little one is very well and very merry......... I should certainly have liked it better if she had been a son, as would Victoria also; but at the same time we must be equally satisfied and thankful as it is......... The rejoicing of the public is universal."

"For a moment only," the Queen says, "was he disappointed at its being a daughter and not a son." His first care, we are told, was for the safety of the Queen, and "we cannot be thankful enough to God," he wrote to the Duchess of Gotha on the 24th, "that everything has passed so very prosperously."

He was ever a most devoted husband and the Queen records that his care of her was like that of a mother

High praise from one who had been blessed with such a mother as the Duchess of Kent.

Two days after the birth of the little Princess, when Mr. Selwyn, a highly distinguished barrister came, as usual, to read law with Prince Albert, the young father said, "I fear I cannot read any law to-day, there are so many constantly coming to congratulate, but you will like to see the little Princess;" and finding that Her Royal Highness was asleep, he took Mr. Selwyn into the nursery, and taking the little hand of the infant, he said,—

"The next time we read, it must be on the rights and duties of a Princess Royal."

A year later, the Prince of Wales came to share his sister's nursery, and then there was great happiness within the palace.

Her Majesty gives us a sketch of a peaceful domestic scene,

"Albert brought in dearest little Pussy (Princess Victoria) in such a smart white merino dress, trimmed with blue, which Mamma had given her and a pretty cap, and placed her on my bed, seating himself next to her, and she was very dear and good; and as my precious invaluable Albert sat there, and our little love between us, I felt quite moved with happiness and gratitude to God."

At Christmas, too, the Queen wrote in her Journal,

"To think that we have two children now, and one who enjoys the sight already (of the Christmas tree); it is like a dream."

Prince Albert, writing to his father, said,—

"This is the dear Christmas Eve on which I have so often listened with impatience for your step, which was to convey us into the gift-room. To-day I have two children of my own to make gifts to, who, they know not why, are full of happy wonder at the German Christmas-tree and its radiant candles."

It was, we are told, "the favourite festival of the Prince—a day he thought for the interchange of presents, as marks of mutual affection and good-will. Christmas-trees were set up in the Queen and Prince's rooms, a custom which was continued in future years, when they were also set up in another room for the young Princes and Princesses, and in the oak-room for the household.

The ladies and gentlemen in waiting were summoned to the corridor on Christmas Eve. The Queen and Prince, accompanied by the Royal Family, pointed out the presents intended for each, inviting them afterwards to go through the different rooms to see what they themselves had mutually given and received."

Writing some weeks after the birth of her little boy, to King Leopold, Her Majesty said:

"I wonder very much whom our little boy will be

like. You will understand how fervent are my prayers, and I am sure everybody's must be, to see him resemble his father in every respect both in mind and body."

And, in another letter, she remarked, "We all have our trials and vexations; but if one's home is happy, then the rest is comparatively nothing."

"In the "Life of Queen Victoria," by Mr. G. Barnett Smith, he mentions that,

"When the baby Prince was a month old the Queen issued a patent creating 'our most dear son' Prince of Wales and Earl of Chester. He was already Duke of Saxony, Duke of Cornwall and Rothesay, Earl of Garrick, Baron of Renfrew, Lord of the Isles, and Great Steward of Scotland. With regard to his new Welsh dignity the patent ran: 'As has been accustomed we do ennoble and invest him with the said principality and Earldom, by girting him with the sword, by putting a coronet on his head and a gold ring on his finger, and also by delivering a gold rod into his hand, that he may preside there and may direct and defend those parts.'.........

The name of Albert was given to the young Prince after his father, and that of Edward, after his maternal grandfather, the Duke of Kent."

CHAPTER XII.

THE QUEEN'S FIRST VISIT TO SCOTLAND.

RECEPTION AT EDINBURGH—ANECDOTES—QUOTATIONS FROM THE QUEEN'S BOOK—LETTERS TO HER MAJESTY'S SCOTTISH SUBJECTS.

THE Queen's first visit to Scotland was made in 1842, with Prince Albert. The young parents left both their little children at home, and Her Majesty records in her book her pleasure at hearing a good account of them from Lady Lyttleton.

The Queen, upon their arrival at Edinburgh yielded to the desire for a State procession, which accordingly took place on the 3rd of September, and was of a most successful and gratifying character. It was described at length in all the English and Scotch papers.

At about half-past ten, Her Majesty set out with Prince Albert from Dalkeith Palace, with the Royal Company of Archers round her carriage, and wearing the Tartan plaid of the Royal Stuart pattern. As she entered the precincts of the Royal grounds a salute was fired from the Castle. The procession moved up the Canongate and the High-Street to the Cross, where the city barrier was erected, amidst the cheers of the people. Here the magistrates were assembled to present the keys of the city to the Sovereign, and the crowd was excessive. At this spot the members of the Celtic Society in the full costume of their respective clans were drawn up. They saluted Her Majesty with their claymores in true Highland fashion, and the Queen made a gracious acknowledgment. The Society then escorted Her Majesty to the Castle.

"The procession halted in front of the Royal Exchange, about fifty yards from the barrier, where the Lord Provost advanced, and, after delivering a brief address, presented the keys of the city to Her Majesty.

"The Queen, after receiving the keys, replied with much dignity mingled with kindness of manner:

"I return the keys of the city with perfect confidence into the safe keeping of the Lord Provost, magistrates and council."

"The procession then resumed its course up the High Street and Lawn market. On entering the esplanade of the Castle Her Majesty was received by the Commander of the Forces, Sir Niel Douglas. Escorted by the Governor and the Fort Major, on either side, and holding the arm of her husband, Her Majesty—(followed by a noble company) walked up the shelving slopes and through the narrow passages which lead to the upper part of the famous fortress, and proceeded to view all that it contained of novelty and interest. She seemed gratified and surprised at the sight of the celebrated gun, "Mons Meg," whose fortunes she appeared perfectly well acquainted with.

"After viewing the magnificent scene over the Firth of Forth from the Mortar Battery, the Queen proceeded to the Half-moon Battery, and thence to the Old Barrack Square. The Crown Jewel Office was next visited, where are deposited the Regalia of Scotland, which, after being lost for a long period, were recovered in 1818, chiefly through the instrumentality of Sir Walter Scott. Her Majesty was much interested in the insignia. Queen Mary's rooms were now visited, and here the Queen was accompanied by Prince Albert only. The chamber in which King James was born Her Majesty regarded with special interest.

"Everything of historical interest having been viewed, the Queen returned to the Castle gate, where she again entered her carriage. Amidst the loud cheering of the multitude she drove down the Castle Hill. In Bank Street there was a dense mass of spectators, and a serious accident occurred owing to the sudden rush of the crowd upon the extensive temporary gallery which had been erected at the foot of the Mound, within the railing at the northernmost angle of the East Princes Street Gardens. Shortly after the Royal procession had passed, the wooden structure gave way with a loud crash, and fifty persons were injured, two of them fatally. In Princes Street and Queensbury Street the crowd was enormous: thousands, who could find no situation from whence a sight of the Sovereign could be obtained, quickly traversed the road through which Her Majesty was to pass until they were fortunate enough to meet with a coign of vantage.

"Sir Thomas Dick Lander has preserved some of the humorous incidents of the Queen's entry into Edinburgh in his memorial of the Sovereign's first visit to Scotland. He states that on Castle Hill an elderly woman succeeded by a *coup de main et de force* in making her way past the guards; and having most unceremoniously passed through the crowd in attendance on Her Majesty, she exclaimed in a convulsive state of excitement, "Oh, will ye no let me see the Queen?

"The military pushed her back, but she was not to be so easily beaten. She again squeezed forward until she stood within a yard of the Royal carriage.

"Hech, sirs," she exclaimed, clasping her hands, "Is that the Queen—is that the Queen! Weel, what have I no seen this day? Eh! but she's a bonnie leddie!"

"The poor woman had not only seen the Queen but she was gratified by the Queen's recognition of herself.*

Another anecdote is told in illustration of the Queen's

---

* Life of Her Majesty Queen Victoria.

quickness of observation and condescension on all such public occasions.

A gentleman who lived near Edinburgh said to his servant on the evening of the Queen's first visit to the city,—

"Well, John, did you see the Queen?"

"Troth did I that, sir."

"Well, what did you think of her, John?"

"Troth, sir, I was terrible feared afore she came forrit—my heart was amaist in my mouth; but when she did come forrit, od, I wasna feared at a'; I just looked at her, an' she looked at me, an' she bowed her heid to me, an' I bowed my heid to her. Od, she's a raal fine leddie, wi' fient a bit o' pride aboot her at a'."

At Dalmeny Park, the residence of the Earl of Roseberry, the Royal party partook of luncheon. It had been arranged that Her Majesty should walk out afterwards in the grounds which command a view of the Forth, the islands that shut it and the heights beyond, but rain fell heavily. However, as a great number of people had assembled on the lawn, Her Majesty went to the library, the windows of which room opened upon the lawn, and advancing to the open window she remained there some time, amidst the loud acclamations of the loyal people.

In the afternoon the Queen and Prince Albert left

Dalmeny Park for Dalkeith, passing through Leith, where Her Majesty stopped to receive a civic address.

The Queen records in her book,—

"The view of *Edinburgh* from the road before you enter *Leith* is quite enchanting; it is, as Albert said, 'fairy like' and what you would only imagine as a thing to dream of, or to see in a picture. There was that beautiful large town, all of stone (no mingled colours of brick to mar it) with the bold castle on one side, and the *Calton Hill* on the other, with those high sharp hills of *Arthur's Seat* and *Salisburg Crags* towering above all and making the finest, boldest back-ground imaginable. Albert said he felt sure the Acropolis could not be finer; and I hear they sometimes call Edinburgh the modern *Athens*."

At Taymouth Castle, the seat of the Marquis of Breadalbane, Her Majesty and Prince Albert met with a brilliant reception.

After gazing upon the scene of it many years afterwards, Her Majesty wrote,—

"We got out and looked from this height down upon the house below, the mist having cleared away sufficiently to show us everything; and then, unknown, quite in private, I gazed—not without deep emotion—on the scene of our reception, twenty-four years ago, by dear Lord Breadalbane, in a princely style, not to be equalled in grandeur and poetic effect.

"Albert and I were then only twenty-three, young and happy. How many are gone that were with us then!"

"*A touch of nature makes the whole world kin,*" and how many of Her Majesty's subjects can enter into her feelings from a similar experience — gazing at the scene of a happy past from the comparative mournfulness of a shadowed present!

Her Majesty thus described the scene,—

"At a quarter to six we reached *Taymouth*. At the gate a guard of Highlanders, Lord Breadalbane's men met us. *Taymouth* lies in a valley surrounded by very high, wooded hills; it is most beautiful. The house is a kind of castle, built of granite. The coup-d'œil was indescribable. There were a number of Lord Breadalbane's Highlanders, all in the Campbell tartan, drawn up in front of the house, with Lord Breadalbane himself in a Highland dress at their head, a few of Sir Neil Menzie's men (in the Menzies red and white tartan) a number of pipers playing, and a company of the 92nd Highlanders, also in kilts. The firing of the guns, the cheering of the great crowd, the picturesqueness of the dresses, the beauty of the surrounding country, with its rich background of wooded hills, altogether formed one of the finest scenes imaginable. Lord and Lady Breadalbane took us upstairs, the hall and stairs being lined with Highlanders............ After dinner, the grounds were most splendidly illuminated, —a whole chain of lamps along the railings, and on the ground was written in lamps, 'Welcome Victoria—Albert.' A small fort, which is up in the woods, was illuminated, and bonfires were burning on the tops of the hills. I never saw anything so fairy-like. There were some pretty fireworks, and the whole ended by Highlanders dancing reels, which they do to perfection, to the sound of the pipes, by torch light, in front of the house. It had a wild and very gay effect."

It is said that on the approach of the Royal party to Taymouth Castle a striking display was made of fine, tall Highlanders in their national costume, and in passing through the Park Her Majesty said to the Marquis:—

"Keeper, what a quantity of fine Highlandmen you have got!" The Royal party stayed some little time at the Castle.

Prince Albert was entertained on the 8th, to a deer-stalking expedition, in which 150 men were engaged, though the Prince was the only person who fired, and he is said to have killed nineteen roe-deer, besides several braces of grouse and other game.

Her Majesty gives us a short extract from one of Prince Albert's letters describing the sport,—

"Without doubt," he said, "deer-stalking is one of the most fatiguing, but it is also one of the most interesting of pursuits. There is not a tree or a bush behind which you can hide yourself............ One has therefore to be constantly on the alert in order to circumvent them; and to keep under the hill out of their wind, crawling on hands and knees, and dressed entirely in grey."

The Queen occupied herself in walking through the gardens of the Castle. She also visited the dairy, and to the surprise and delight of the women in charge, had some milk and a piece of bread. The amusements were continued on the 9th, and in the evening a ball was given which Her Majesty opened with the Duke of Buccleuch and the Prince with the Duchess.

Previously to leaving Taymouth Castle, on the 10th, Her Majesty planted a fir and an oak tree in the grounds as a memorial of her visit.

Two days afterwards, when the Queen was staying at Drummond Castle as the guest of Lord and Lady Willoughby D'Eresby, a picturesque scene took place.

A hundred Highlanders in the Drummond tartan, some armed with Lochaber axes, others with swords and bucklers, paraded before Her Majesty. "An old man known as Comrie of Comrie, who claimed to be hereditary standard-bearer of the Perth family, displayed the very flag which had been rescued by his great-uncle after it had been taken by King George's troops at the Battle of Culloden; and he also wore the same claymore which did service on that occasion."

An interesting story is told us of the Prince Consort, when he was deer-stalking at Drummond Castle under the able guidance of Campbell of Moonzie.

"Prince Albert had arranged to return at a particular hour to drive with the Queen. Moonzie, who was the most ardent and agile deer-stalker in the neighbourhood, had got into the swing of the sport, till then unsuccessful, when, as the men lay crouching among the heather, waiting intently for the herd expected to come that way, the Prince said it was time to return.

'But the deer, your Royal Highness,' faltered the Highlander, looking aghast and speaking in a whisper, which the exigencies of the case required.

The Prince explained that the Queen expected him.

It is to be feared the Highlander, in the excitement of the moment, and the marvel that any man—not to say any Prince—could give up the sport at such a crisis, suggested that the Queen might wait, while the deer certainly would not.

'The Queen commands,' said her true knight, with a quiet smile and a gentle rebuke."

On the 13th the Queen and Prince left Drummond Castle on their return journey. On reaching Viscount Strathallan's estate Her Majesty passed under a beautiful arch, over which the words were inscribed,

"Adieu! fair daughter of Strathearn." in allusion to the title of the Queen's father as Duke of Kent and Strathearn.

"That the Queen honoured the memory of that dear father whom she could not remember, the following little incident shows plainly.

"At Stirling, the Provost, in receiving Her Majesty, mentioned that he had the honour to serve under the Duke of Kent for twenty-four years.

"The Queen was quite delighted and said: 'It gives me great satisfaction to meet, in a Provost of this town, one who has served under my revered father.'"

We are told that Her Majesty was, altogether, so much impressed with the heartiness of her reception by all classes of her Northern subjects that, before leaving Scotland, she caused the Earl of Aberdeen to write;—

"The Queen cannot leave Scotland without a feeling of regret that her visit on the present occasion could not be further prolonged. Her Majesty fully expected to witness the loyalty and attachment of her Scottish subjects; but the devotion and enthusiasm evinced in every quarter, and by all ranks, have produced an impression on the mind of Her Majesty which can never be effaced."

CHAPTER XIII.

MORE ABOUT THE ROYAL CHILDREN.

THE LITTLE PRINCESS ROYAL—THE LITTLE PRINCE OF WALES—LADY BLOOM-
FIELD'S REMINISCENCES—THE PRINCESS ROYAL TRAVELLING IN SCOTLAND
WITH HER PARENTS—STAYING AT BLAIR ATHOLE—ANECDOTE OF THE
QUEEN—OTHER INCIDENTS OF LIFE IN THE HIGHLANDS.

LESLIE wrote in his "Recollections." "In 1841, I painted a second picture for the Queen, the christening of the Princess Royal. I was admitted to see the ceremony, and made a slight sketch of the Royal personages as they stood round the font in the room. I made a study from the little Princess a few days afterwards. She was then three months old, a finer child of that age I never saw."

The Princess Royal was a remarkably quick and intelligent child; when she was only three years old Her Majesty recorded,

"Our *Pussy* learns a verse of Lamartine by heart which ends with '*Le tableau se déroule à mes pieds*' (The picture spreads itself at my feet). To show you how well she understood this difficult line, I must tell you the following *bon mot*. When she was riding on her pony, and looking at the cows and sheep, she turned to Madame Charnier (her governess) and said, "*Voila le tableau qui se déroule à mes pieds!*" (There is the picture which spreads itself at my feet.) Is not this extraordinary for a child of three?"*

The Princess Royal was bright and lively, Miss Tytler says, and the Prince of Wales a beautiful good-tempered baby, and both children were fond of music, as the children of such musical parents might well be. "When the youthful pair were a little older they would stand, still and quiet, in the music-room to hear the Prince-father discourse sweet sounds on his organ, and the Queen-mother sing with one of her ladies 'in perfect time and tune,' with a fine feeling for her songs, as Mendelssohn has described her. The small people furnished a never-ending series of merry anecdotes and witticisms all their own, and would have gone far to break down the highest dead wall of stiffness and reserve, had such a barrier ever existed." Then the writer mentions "the little Princess, a quaint tiny figure 'in dark blue velvet and white shoes, and yellow kid gloves,' keeping the nurseries alive with her sports, showing off the new frocks she had got as a Christmas-box from her grandmamma the Duchess of Kent, and bidding Miss Liddel put on one."

---

* "The Queen's Resolve," by Rev. C. Bullock.

In Lady Bloomfield's "*Reminiscences of Court and Diplomatic Life*," she wrote:—

"*Windsor Castle, Aug.* 12*th*, 1843,—I had a delightful ride with the Queen yesterday, who most kindly lent me her habit, hat, collar and cuffs. Considering the great difference in our figures, the habit fitted me wonderfully......... We rode all about the Park for two hours and a quarter and I never enjoyed anything more. I do hope the Queen will continue to ride, because as neither Lady Dunmore nor Matilda Paget ever do, I shall probably always have to accompany Her Majesty. No one dined here last night, so we talked a great deal to the Queen, and afterwards played at *vingt-et-un*................

The Queen told us a funny anecdote of the little Princess Royal. Whilst they were driving the other day, the Queen called her as she often does "Missy." The Princess took no notice the first time, but the next she looked up very indignantly, and said to her mother, "I'm not Missy, I'm the Princess Royal." She speaks French fluently, and she was reading the other day when Lady Lyttleton went up to her; so she motioned her away with her hand, saying,

"*N 'approchez pas moi, moi ne veut pas vous.*"

(Do not approach me, I do not want you.)

"The Duchess of Kent very kindly sent me an immense heap of music yesterday, vocal and instrumental.

I delight in looking over new music. We took a long drive, and the more I see of this lovely Park, the more I admire it; the scene varies so much, that almost every day I become acquainted with fresh beauties. The Queen went with the little Princess and the Duchess of Buccleuch in one of the small ponycarriages, and before we started there was a little delay, so I witnessed a most interesting scene between the Duke of Wellington and the Princess. She looked at him very hard, and he bent down in the most gallant manner and kissed her tiny hand, and told her to remember him, as well she may. The Duke is looking very well and rode part of the way with us, but he refrained from accompanying us all the time we drove, for the Queen drives so fast, it is very hard work riding by her carriage."

Again Lady Bloomfield wrote,—

"August 26th—we drove with the Queen and the little Princess yesterday. The latter chattered the whole time and was very amusing. Prince Albert rode away to look at a house he is having built, and the carriage stood still until he returned. The Queen was talking to us and not taking any notice of the Princess, who suddenly exclaimed, "There's a cat under the trees,"—fertile imagination on her part, as there was nothing of the kind, but, having succeeded in attracting attention, she quietly said, "Cat come out to look at the Queen, I suppose."

Then she took a fancy to some heather at the side of the road and asked Lady Dunmore to get her some. Lady Dunmore replied that she could not do that, as we were driving too fast; so the Princess answered, "No, you can't, but *those girls* might get out and get me some,"—meaning Miss Paget and me. "The two Maids of Honour in the full dignity of their nineteen or twenty summers and of their office."

Later in the year Lady Bloomfield wrote,—

"Windsor Castle, December 15th, 1843.—I went to the Queen's room yesterday, and saw her before we began to sing. She was so thoroughly kind and gracious. The music went off very well. Costa (Sir Michael) accompanied, and I was pleased by the Queen's telling me, when I asked her whether I had not better practise the things a little more, that "that was not necessary as I knew them perfectly." She also said, "If it was convenient to me I was to go down to her room any evening to try the *Masses*." Just as if anything she desired could be *inconvenient!*.........

"We had a pleasant interview with the Royal children in Lady Lyttleton's room yesterday, and *almost* a romp with the little Princess Royal and the Prince of Wales. They had got a round ivory counter, which I spun for them, and they went into such fits of laughter it did my heart good to hear them. The Princess Royal is wonderfully quick and clever. She is always in the Queen's room when we play or sing and she seems especially fond of music, and stands listening most attentively without moving.

"December 18th,—We walked with the Queen and Prince yesterday to the Home Farm, saw the turkeys crammed, looked at the pigs, and then went to see the new aviary, where there is a beautiful collection of pigeons, fowls, &c., of rare kinds. The pigeons are so tame they will perch upon Prince Albert's hat and the Queen's shoulders. It was funny seeing the Royal pair amusing themselves with farming!

"December 19th.— My waiting is nearly over, and though I shall be delighted to get home, I always regret leaving my dear kind mistress, particularly when I have been a good deal with Her Majesty as I have this waiting. We sang again last night, and after Costa went away, I sorted a quantity of music for the Queen; and then Prince Albert said he had composed a German ballad, which he thought would suit my voice, and he wished me to sing it. So His Royal Highness accompanied me, and I sang it at sight, which rather alarmed me; but I got through it, and it is very pretty. The Duchess of Kent has promised to have it copied for me. The Prince of Wales stayed some time in the room while we were practising. He was very attentive, and both he and the Princess Royal seem to have a decided taste for music. We sang some of my beloved Masses (Mozart's), and you cannot think how beautiful they are with all the parts filled up. Costa had composed a very pretty Miserere, which we also sang."

When the Queen was travelling round the shores of Scotland in her yacht, she used to give the little Princess Royal a lesson and would hear her read in her history-book herself, and once we find her lamenting that she had not always time to hear her say her daily prayers.

This was the first journey of the little Princess with her Royal mother, who tells us how "Vicky stood and bowed to the people out of the window." The little lady was then not quite four years old.

The Prince of Wales, the Princess Alice and the baby, Prince Alfred, (at that time five weeks old) were left at home, and only our Queen's elder daughter accompanied her parents. Her Majesty tells us that at Dundee,—"At half-past eight we got into our barge with Vicky, and our ladies and gentlemen. The sea was bright and blue; the boat danced along beautifully. We had about a quarter of a mile to row.

"A staircase covered with red cloth, was arranged for us to land upon, and there were a great many people; but everything was so well arranged that all crowding was avoided, and only the magistrates were below the platform where the people were. Albert walked up the steps with me, I holding his arm and Vicky his hand, amidst the loud cheers of the people, all the way to the carriage, our dear Vicky behaving like a grown up person — not put out, nor frightened, nor nervous. We got into our postchaise, and, at the same time, Renwick took Vicky up in his arms and put her in the next carriage with her governess and nurse.

"There was a great crowd in Dundee, but everything was very well managed, and there would have been no crowding at all, had not, as usual, about twenty people begun to run along with the carriage, and thus forced a number of others to follow.

"About three miles beyond *Dundee* we stopped at the gate of Lord Camperdown's place; here a triumphal arch had been erected, and Lady Camperdown and Lady Duncan and her little boy, with others, were all waiting to welcome us and were very civil and kind. The little boy, beautifully dressed in the Highland dress, was carried to Vicky, and gave her a basket with fruit and flowers.

"I said to Albert I could hardly believe that our child was travelling with us—it put me so in mind of myself when I was the "little Princess." Albert observed that it was always said that parents lived their lives over again in their children, which is a very pleasant feeling."

Again Her Majesty, speaking of the Princess, said, "There never was such a good traveller as she is, sleeping in the carriage at her usual times, not put out, not frightened at noise or crowds; but pleased and amused. She never heard the anchor go at night on board ship; but slept as sound as a top."

Her Majesty had intimated this time that she had gone to the North for the purpose of enjoying a period of strict quietude and seclusion, and she devoted herself to the rural recreations which had such a charm for both herself and her husband. The chroniclers of the time, however, enable us to catch several glimpses of the Queen's doings. Thus we find it was Her Majesty's habit to rise with the sun, and to take very early walks with the Prince Consort and the Princess Royal. "Vicky" always rode her Shetland pony when she accompanied her parents on these occasions, but Prince Albert would sometimes take her in his arms and point out any object which would attract the wondering fancy of the child.

"Pussy's cheeks are on the point of bursting, they have grown so red and plump," the Prince wrote to his step-mother. "She is learning Gaelic, but makes wild work with the names of the mountains."

The Queen's piper, Mackay, who attended her during

her stay at Blair Athole, had orders to play the pibroch under Her Majesty's window every morning at seven o'clock; and, at the same time, a bunch of fresh heather, with some of the icy cold water from the famous spring of Glen Tilt, were presented to the Queen.

One of the local journals published the following characteristic anecdote :—

"One morning about seven o'clock, a lady plainly dressed left the Castle; who, though observed by the Highland guard on duty, was allowed to pass unnoticed, until after she had proceeded for a considerable distance; when some one having discovered that it was the Queen, a party of the Highlanders turned out as a Royal body-guard. Her Majesty, however, signified her wish to dispense with their services, and they all returned to their stations. The Queen, in the meanwhile, moved onwards through the Castle grounds, perfectly alone, until she reached the lodge, the temporary residence of Lord and Lady Glenlyon; where, upon calling with the intention, as was understood, of making some arrangements for a preconcerted excursion to the Falls of Bruar, she was informed that his lordship had not yet risen. The surprise of the domestic may be conceived when Her Majesty announced who was to be intimated as having called upon his lordship.

"On her return, Her Majesty having taken a different route, and finding herself bewildered by the various roads which intersect the grounds in every direction, applied to some reapers whom she met to direct her to the Castle by the nearest way. They, not being aware to whom they spoke, immediately did so, by directing Her Majesty across one of the parks, and over a paling that lay before her—which she at once climbed over, and reached the Castle—a good deal amused, no doubt, with her morning's excursion."

One fine September morning Prince Albert and the Queen rode on a dun and a grey pony, attended only by Sandy McAra, who led the Queen's pony through the ford, up the hill of Tulloch, "to the very top." There they saw a whole circle of stupendous Bens— Ben Vrackie, Ben-y-Ghlo, Ben-y-Chat, and the Falls of the Bruar and the Pass of Killie Krankie.

"It was quite romantic," said the Queen. "Here we were with only this Highlander behind us holding the ponies—for we got off twice and walked about; not a house, not a creature near us, but the pretty Highland sheep, with their horns and black faces, up to the top of Tulloch, surrounded by beautiful mountains.........the most delightful, the most romantic ride I ever had."

Miss Tytler tells us, "There was much more riding and driving in Glen Tilt, with its disputed 'right of way' case, but there was none to bar the Queen's progress. Her Majesty showed herself a fearless rider, abandoning the cart-roads and following the foot-tracks among the mountains. She grew as fond of her homely Highland pony, *Arghait Bhean*, with which Lord Glenlyon supplied her, as she was of her Windsor stud with every trace of high breeding in their small heads, arching necks, slender legs and dainty hoofs.

One day the foresters succeeded in driving a great herd of red deer, with their magnificent antlers, across the heights, so that the Queen had a passing view of them. On another day she was able to join in the deer-stalking; scrambling for hours in the wake of the hunters, among the rocks and heather, when she was not "allowed" as she described it, to speak above a whisper, in case she should spoil the sport. It was a brief taste of an ideal open-air, unsophisticated life, upon which there was no intrusion, except when stolid sight-seers flocked to the little parish Church of Blair Athole for the chance of seeing Royalty............ The Queen, as usual, enjoyed and admired everything there was to admire—the pretty jackets, or "short gowns" of the rustic maidens; the "burns," clear as glass; the mossy stones; the peeps between the trees; the depth of the shadows; the corn-cutting or "shearing," when a patch of yellow oats broke the purple shadow of the moor, &c., &c."

Prince Albert, who had always, as we have already noticed, been an ardent admirer of natural scenery was, also delighted with the beauties of nature all around them, and with their free and unsophisticated mountain-life. But the visit drew to an end all too soon, and the Royal pair had to return to the splendour and ceremonials of State life.

CHAPTER XIV.

VERY DIFFERENT SCENES.

VISIT FROM THE KING LOUIS PHILIPPE OF FRANCE—HIS RECEPTION—DRIVING OUT WITH THE QUEEN—INVESTITURE WITH THE GARTER.

THE Queen and Prince, we are told, returned to Windsor to receive a visit from Louis Philippe. The King, who had spent part of his exiled youth in England, had not been there since 1815, when he had been taking refuge there, after Napoleon's return from Elba and Louis the Eighteenth's withdrawal to Ghent, till the Battle of Waterloo restored the heads of the Bourbon and Orleans families to the Tuilleries and the Palais Royal.

The King arrived at Portsmouth on the 6th of October, accompanied by his son and a numerous suite. The Corporation came on board to present an address to which the King replied in English, with much effusion and affability, shaking hands with all the magistrates, and telling those who were too slow in removing their white gloves, "Oh, never mind your gloves, gentlemen." Prince Albert and the Duke of Wellington went on board, and the enthusiastic visitor saluted the Prince on the cheek, but he contented himself with shaking hands.

The Queen met her guest in the grand vestibule fronting George the Fourth's Gate at Windsor Castle; the Duchess of Kent, the ladies of the household, Sir Robert Peel and the officers of the household being with Her Majesty. The moment the carriage drew up, the Queen advanced and extended her arms to her father's old friend. The two Sovereigns embraced, and Her Majesty led the way to the suite of rooms which the King was to have during his stay.

Lady Lyttleton wrote of the event,—

"At two o'clock he arrived, this curious King, worth seeing, if ever a body was. The Queen having graciously permitted me to be present, I joined the Court in the Corridor, and we waited an hour, and then the Queen of England came out of her room to go and receive the King of France—the first time in history! Her Majesty had not long to wait—and, from the armoury amidst all the old trophies and knight's armour, and Nelson's bust, and Marlborough's flag, and Wellington's, we saw the first of the escort enter the Quadrangle, and down flew the Queen, and we after her, to the outside of the door on the pavement of the Quadrangle, just in time to see the escort clattering up, and the carriage close behind. The old man was much moved, I think, and his hand rather shook as he alighted, his hat quite off and grey hair seen. His countenance is striking — much better than his portraits — and his embrace of the Queen was very parental and nice. — It was a striking bit of real history, made one think and feel much."

"He is the first King of France who comes on a visit to the Sovereign of this country," wrote the Queen in her Journal......... "The King said, as he went up the grand staircase to his apartments, 'How beautiful!' .... I never saw anybody more pleased or more amused in looking at every picture, every bust. He knew every bust, and knew everything about everybody here in a most wonderful way. Such a memory! Such activity! It is a pleasure to show him anything, as he is so pleased and interested. He is enchanted with the Castle, and repeated to me again and again (as did also his people) how delighted he was to be here; how he had feared that what he had so earnestly wished since I came to the throne would not take place, and — 'What a pleasure it is to me to give you my arm!'"

On the 8th of the month the Queen took her visitor on a little pilgrimage to Claremont and Twickenham, to the house in which he had resided as Duc D'Orléans. The Queen wrote, —

"We proceeded by Staines, where the King recognised

the inn and everything, to Twickenham, where we drove up to the house where he used to live, and where Lord and Lady Mornington, who received us, are now living. It is a very pretty house, much embellished since the King lived there, but otherwise much the same, and he seemed greatly pleased to see it again. He walked round the garden, in spite of the heavy shower which had just fallen......... The King himself directed the postilion which way to go to pass by the house where he lived for five years with his poor brothers, before his marriage........."

Speaking of their conversation during the great banquet which wound up the proceedings of the day, Her Majesty wrote, " He talked to me of the time when he was in a school in the Grisons, a teacher merely, receiving twenty pence a day, having to brush his own boots, and under the name of Chabot. What an eventful life his has been!"

On the 9th, the King was invested with the Order of the Garter. Sir Theodore Martin wrote, in respect of this ceremony, "It must have been pregnant with associations to all present who remembered that the Order had been instituted by Edward III., after the Battle of Cressy, and that its earliest knights were the Black Prince and his companions, whose prowess had been so fatal to France."

Her Majesty, who was attired in the (blue velvet)

mantle of the Order, its motto inscribed on a bracelet that encircled her arm, and a diamond tiara on her head, with Prince Albert invested the King, who was dressed in a uniform of dark blue and gold, with the Garter.

Her Majesty wrote, "Albert then placed the Garter round the King's leg, I pulled it through while the admonition was being read, and the King said to me 'I wish to kiss this hand,' which he did afterwards, and I embraced him."

Afterwards, taking the King's arm, Her Majesty conducted him in state to his apartment.

"At four o'clock," the Queen wrote, "we again went over to the King's room, and I placed at his feet a large cup representing St. George and the dragon, with which he was very much pleased."

In the evening there was a splendid banquet in St. George's Hall to commemorate the instalment.

It was, when the Prince and Queen accompanied the King part of the way on his return journey, and after they had parted from him, that they went to see the house and grounds of Osborne which were to be sold. Sir Robert Peel had suggested that they were exactly constituted to form the retired, yet not too distant, country and seaside home for which the Royal couple were looking out.

CHAPTER XV.

OSBORNE.

OSBORNE—SIR CHARLES LYELL'S NOTES OF A VISIT THERE—THE CHILDREN'S WORKPLACE AND PLAY GROUND.

IT is in the nature of work that it should grow, and, as the cares and responsibilities of life increased and settled more and more heavily upon the Prince and Queen, they felt increasing need of a place of retirement, where they might be free from the trammels and ceremonies of State life, and be able to devote more time to the personal supervision of their children.

In our book, "Scenes in the Life of the Princess Alice," we have related how first Osborne and then Balmoral were chosen to be the homes of the Royal Family. It is not our purpose, therefore, now, to enter into the interesting particulars of how these places were selected and approved of by the Prince and Queen, and how, eventually, they were filled with their happy occupants.

Before Osborne was obtained for a Royal residence the only marine one the Prince and Queen had possessed was the Pavilion at Brighton, where it was impossible for them to be in the privacy and seclusion which they desired.

Her Majesty, writing of Osborne in 1845, said "It sounds so pleasant to have a place of one's own, quiet and retired, and free from all woods and forests and other charming departments, which really are the plague of one's life. It is impossible to see a prettier place, with woods, and valleys, and points of view, which would be beautiful anywhere; but when these are combined with the sea (to which the woods grow down) and a beach which is quite private, it is really everything one could wish."

Sir Charles Lyell had the honour of paying a visit to Osborne some years later, and, in his "*Life*," there are some interesting particulars of the Queen and the Royal Family. He writes,

"It is a very pleasant residence; like a small German principality palace......... The Prince invited us to join the ladies and sit down at their table, and I was asked by the Queen news of New York doings, and made them merry with Soft Shell, Old Hunkers, &c., and gave them an account of the Exhibition prospects, United States prosperity, &c.."......... "The Queen told me that her sons had asked her if Colenso, whose arithmetic they had studied, was the Bishop; and had remarked, "Then he must be very clever."

"I said that my nephew Arthur had said, 'I don't like Colenso; he gives me hard sums to do.'

"She laughed, and, asking his age, said, 'All mine were older.'

"At Balmoral.—The day I went to dine there, Saturday last, I had first a long walk—Sir James Clark and I—with Mr. Birch (the tutor of the Prince of Wales) and his pupil, a pleasing lively boy, whose animated description of the conjuror, or wizard of the North, whom they had seen a few days before was very amusing. 'He (the wizard) had cut to pieces Mamma's pocket-handkerchief, then darned it and ironed it, so that it was as entire as ever, he had fired a pistol, and caused five or six watches to go through Gibbs's (one of their footmen) head, and all were tied to a chair on Gibbs's other side,' and so forth, 'but Papa (Prince Albert,) knows how all these things are done, and had the watches really gone through Gibbs's head he could hardly have looked so well, though he was confounded.' Sometimes I walked alone with the child who asked me the names of plants, and to let him see spiders, &c., through my magnifying glass, sometimes with the tutor, whom I continue to like more as I become better acquainted. After our ramble of two hours and a half through some wild scenery, I was sent for to join another party, where I found the Queen, Prince and

Lord John by a deep pool on the river Dee, fishing for trout and salmon.

"After the Queen had entered the Castle the Prince kept me so long, and we kept one another so late, talking on all kinds of subjects, that a messenger came from Her Majesty saying it was only a quarter of an hour to dinner-time.

"After the ladies had gone to the drawing-room we had much lively talk, which the Prince promoted greatly, telling some amusing stories himself, and encouraging others by laughing at theirs.

"Next day I went to Church. The prayer for the parish, magistracy, Queen and Royal family, judges, ministers of religion, Parliament, and whole nation was just such as you would have liked and in excellent taste, with nothing which a republican jealous of equality could, I think, have objected to, and which I believe our Sovereign and her husband would thoroughly appreciate the simplicity of. They shoved the box on the end of a long pole to the Queen and Prince, and maids of honour, as to all the rest of the congregation, and each dropped in their piece of coin. After Church I had much conversation alone with Prince Albert, whose mind is in full activity on a variety of grave subjects, while he is invigorating his body with field sports.

"We are told that perhaps Osborne more than any of the homes of the Royal Family was the play-place and school of the children. The Queen often refers to the 'Island home,' where they were wholly given up to the enjoyment of the warm summer weather, when the Queen sat under the trees, and the children were catching butterflies."

At Osborne was the small fortress, complete in all its details, which was entirely erected by the hands of the young Princes. And there, too, was the Swiss Cottage which was used by the Prince as a museum and school of practical science and industry in the education of the Royal children. There, too, as we have mentioned elsewhere,[*] the Royal children had each their own flower and vegetable garden, hot-house and forcing-frame. Each had a set of tools and the Princes had a carpenter's shop, in which they worked with great zeal and earnestness. In the cottage, the ground floor was fitted up as kitchen, with pantry, &c., &c., and there the young Princesses might have been seen with their sleeves rolled up and arms bare, deep in the mysteries of pastry-making, cooking and all those useful domestic duties which it is wise for every mistress of a household to thoroughly understand. Years afterwards, we read of one of those Princesses, (Princess Alice,) in the land of her adoption, helping a poor man with her own hands, to "cook something" for his sick wife. And we are told the young Princesses delighted

---
[*] "Scenes in the Life of the Princess Alice."

THE ROYAL FAMILY.

to invite their parents to come and partake of what they had themselves prepared; or, doubtless oftener, they would distribute the result of their handiwork amongst the poor of the neighbourhood.

They must have been very happy children, for we read that, years later, the Princess Royal, then the Crown Princess of Germany, and the Princess Louis of Hesse talked over their childhood together, with the result, said the latter, that if the Queen and their father could have heard them they would have been quite repaid for all the trouble they had taken about them when they were little ones.

CHAPTER XVI.

BALMORAL.

EXTRACTS FROM FIRST LETTERS OF THE PRINCE AND QUEEN FROM BALMORAL—DEER-STALKING—READING AND QUOTING POETRY—ACCOUNT OF THE SCOTCH HOME IN GREVILLE'S JOURNAL—HER MAJESTY'S VISIT TO POOR OLD WOMEN.

THREE years afterwards, Balmoral, which is perhaps our Queen's favourite residence, was taken possession of by her and the Prince.

The latter writing of it that year, 1848, said,—

"We have withdrawn for a short time into a complete mountain solitude, where one rarely sees a human face, where the snow already covers the mountain tops, and the wild deer come creeping stealthily round the house......... This place belonged to poor Sir Robert Gordon, Lord Aberdeen's brother, and the little castle was built by him. It is of granite, with numerous small turrets, and whitewashed, and is situated upon a rising ground, surrounded by birch-wood and close to the river Dee. The air is glorious and clear, but icy cold."

The Queen wrote about the same time, "We walked

THE ROYAL FAMILY. 183

out, and went up to the top of the wooded hill opposite our windows, where there is a cairn, and up which is a pretty winding path. The view from here looking down upon the house is charming. To the left you look towards the beautiful hills surrounding *Loch-na-Gar*, and to the right towards *Ballatar*, to the glen (or valley) along which the Dee winds, with beautiful wooded hills, which reminded us very much of the Thüringerwald. It was so calm, and so solitary, it did one good as one gazed around; and the pure mountain air was most refreshing.

"All seemed to breathe freedom and peace, and to make one forget the world and its sad turmoils. The scenery is wild, and yet not desolate; and everything looks much more prosperous and cultivated than at *Laggan*. Then the soil is delightfully dry. We walked beside the Dee, a beautiful rapid stream, which is close behind the house. The view of the hills towards *Invercauld* is exceedingly fine."

In Her Majesty's two books, she gives us many other interesting glimpses of the—

> Land of brown heath and shaggy wood,
> Land of the mountain and the flood,

As, for instance, the following graphic account of a "Drive" in the *Balloch Buie* in September of the same year, 1848.

"At a quarter past ten o'clock we set off in a post-chaise with Bertie (the Prince of Wales), and drove beyond the house of Mr. Farquharson's keeper in the *Balloch Buie*. We then mounted our ponies, Bertie riding Grant's pony on the deer-saddle, and being led by a gillie, Grant walking by his side. Macdonald and several gillies were with us, and we were preceded by Bowman and old Arthur Farquharson, a deer-stalker of Invercaulds. They took us up a beautiful path winding through the trees and heather in the *Balloch Buie;* but when we had got about a mile or more they discovered deer. A 'council of war' was held in a whisper, and we turned back and went the whole way down again, and rode along to the keeper's lodge, where we turned up the glen immediately below *Craig Daign*, through a beautiful part of the wood, and went on along the track, till we came to the foot of the craig, where we all dismounted.

"We scrambled up an almost perpendicular place where there was a little *box*, made of hurdles and interwoven with branches of fir and heather, about five feet in height. There we seated ourselves with Bertie, Macdonald lying in the heather near us watching and quite concealed; some had gone round to beat, and others again were at a little distance. We sat quite still and sketched a little; I doing the landscape and some trees, Albert drawing Macdonald as he lay there.

This lasted for nearly an hour, when Albert fancied he heard a distant sound, and, in a few minutes, Macdonald whispered that he saw stags, and that Albert should wait and take a steady aim. We then heard them coming past. Albert did not look over the box, but through it; and fired through the branches, and then again over the box. The deer retreated; but Albert felt certain he had hit a stag. He ran up to the keepers, and at that moment they called from below that they 'had got him,' and Albert ran on to see. I waited for a bit; but soon scrambled on with Bertie and Macdonald's help; and Albert joined me directly, and we all went down and saw a magnificent stag, 'a royal,' which had dropped soon after Albert had hit him, at one of the men's feet. The sport was successful and everyone was delighted, — Macdonald and the keepers in particular;—the former saying, 'that it was Her Majesty's coming out that had brought the good luck.' I was supposed to have a 'lucky foot of which the Highlanders think a great deal.'"

Again, in 1852, on the last day of their stay that year at Balmoral, after they had all been helping to build the Cairn at *Craig Gowan** Her Majesty writes,

"After luncheon, Albert decided to walk through the woods for a last chance, and allowed Vicky and me to go with him. At half-past three o'clock we started,

---

* For particulars of that see our "Scenes in the Life of the Princess Alice."

got out at Grant's, and walked up part of *Carrop*, intending to go along the upper path, when a stag was heard to roar, and we all turned into the wood. We crept along, and got into the middle path. Albert soon left us to go lower, and we sat down to wait for him: presently we heard a shot—then complete silence—and after another pause of some little time, three more shots. This was again succeeded by complete silence. We sent some one to look, who shortly after returned, saying the stag had been twice hit and they were after him. Macdonald next went, and in about five minutes we heard "Soloman" give tongue and knew he had the stag at bay. We listened a little while, and then began moving down hoping to arrive in time; but the barking had ceased and Albert had already killed the stag; and on the road he lay, a little way beyond *Invergelder* —the beauty that we had admired yesterday evening. He was a magnificent animal, and I sat down and scratched a little scrap of him on a bit of paper that Macdonald had in his pocket, which I put on a stone —while Albert and Vicky, with the others, built a little cairn to mark the spot. We heard, after I had finished my little scrawl and the carriage had joined us that another stag had been seen near the road; and we had not gone as far as the "Irons" before we saw one below the road looking so handsome. Albert jumped out and fired—the animal fell but rose again, and went on a little way, and Albert followed. Very shortly after we heard a cry, and ran down and found Grant and Donald Stewart, the stag and the dogs. I sat down to sketch, and poor Vicky, unfortunately sat down on a wasp's nest, and was much stung. Donald Stewart rescued her, for I could not, being myself too much alarmed. Albert joined us in twenty minutes, unaware of having killed the stag. What a delightful day! But sad that it should be our last day! Home by half-past six. We found our beautiful stag had arrived, and admired him much."

At one time we find the Queen and Prince Consort reading Scott's picturesque poems together, another time Her Majesty quotes Clough's inimitable description of an October day, in his *Bothie of Tober-na-Vuolich*, it is so beautiful that we must give the extract here, only adding that the Queen said it admirably pourtrayed what she saw,—

"The gorgeous bright October,
Then when brackens are changed, and heather blooms
   are faded,
And amid russet of heather and ferns, green trees are bonnie;
Alders are green, and oaks; the rowan scarlet and yellow;
One great glory of broad gold pieces appears the aspen,
And the jewels of gold that were hung in the hair of
   the birch-tree,
Pendulons, here and there, her coronet, necklace, and
   earrings,
Cover her now, o'er and o'er; she is weary and scatters them
   from her."

And again, another time, the Queen gives us a long extract from the thoughtful and beautiful writings of the Rev. F. W. Robertson. His description of a Tyrolese being, said Her Majesty, even more applicable to a Highlander.

With such thoughtful, cultured tastes as Her Majesty and the Prince Consort possessed, in their beautiful mountain home, surrounded by their happy family, we can imagine many an interesting and beautiful scene.

We are told that "The Royal Family, perfectly free from all restraint, were engaged in reading, sketching, painting, etching, photography, and gardening, each trying to out-do the other in seeking to reach some practical end; and all in the buoyancy of real filial affection, which blends the best sympathies of parental love. At Balmoral the Queen appeared, not in her regal character, but as the mother; while the Prince, as the head of the family, was looked up to and loved with the tenderest emotion."

Greville gives us a picturesque account of their Scotch home in his *Journal*, he writes,

"They live there without any state whatever; they live not merely like private gentlefolks, but like very small gentlefolks—small house, small rooms, small establishment. There are no soldiers, and the whole guard of the Sovereign and the whole Royal Family is a single policeman, who walks about the grounds to keep off impertinent intruders or improper characters. Their attendants consisted of Lady Douro and Miss Dawson, lady and maid of honour; George Anson and Gordon; Birch, the Prince of Wales tutor, and Miss Hildyard, the governess of the children. They live with the greatest simplicity and ease. The Prince shoots every morning, returns to luncheon, and then they walk and drive. The Queen is running in and out of the house all day long, and often goes about alone, walks into the cottages, and sits down and chats with the old women.

"I never before was in society with the Prince, or had any conversation with him. On Thursday morning John Russell and I were sitting together after breakfast, when he came in and sat down with us, and we conversed for about three quarters of an hour. I was greatly struck with him. I saw at once (what I had always heard) that he is very intelligent and highly cultivated, and, moreover, that he has a thoughtful mind, and thinks of subjects worth thinking about. He seemed very much at his ease, very gay, pleasant, and without the least stiffness or air of dignity. After luncheon, we went to the Highland gathering at Braemar —the Queen, the Prince, four children, and two ladies in one pony carriage; John Russell, Miss Hildyard, Mr. Birch and I in another; Angus and Gordon on the box; one groom, no more. The gathering was at the Castle of Braemar, and a pretty sight enough. We returned as we came, and then everybody strolled about till dinner. We were only nine people, and it was all very easy and really agreeable, the Queen in very good humour and talkative; the Prince still more so, and talking very well; no form and everybody seemed at their ease."

It is well known what a happy thing it was for the poor, both at Osborne and at Balmoral, when Her Majesty and Prince Consort came to dwell among them. We are told, "To care for those who, either as tenants or labourers, lived on the estate, and so to attach them more and more to the land and its owners, was their first thought."

And again,

"To increase the comforts of his tenants, to elevate their moral and social condition, were objects already kept in view from the time the Prince became a proprietor of Highland property; and they were pursued with unabated zeal to the end of his life."

Her Majesty herself gives us an account of some of her visits to the poor at Balmoral. The time was shortly before her eldest daughter the Princess Royal was married, and, as we shall see, touching allusions were made to the great event by the poor old women. Her Majesty wrote,

"Saturday, September 26, 1857.

"Albert went out with Alfred for the day, and I

walked out with the two girls and Lady Churchill, stopped at the shop and made some purchases for poor people and others; drove a little way, got out and walked up the hill to Balnacroft, Mrs. P. Farquharson's, and she walked round with us to some of the cottages to show me where the poor people lived, and to tell them who I was. Before we went into any we met an old woman, who, Mrs. Farquharson said, was very poor, eighty-eight years old, and mother to the former distiller. I gave her a warm petticoat, and the tears rolled down her old cheeks, and she shook my hands, and prayed God to bless us: it was very touching.

"I went into a small cabin of old Kitty Kear's, who is eighty-six years old—quite erect, and who welcomed us with a great air of dignity. She sat down and spun. I gave her, also, a warm petticoat; she said, 'May the Lord ever attend ye and yours, here, and hereafter; and may the Lord be a guide to ye, and keep ye from all harm.' She was quite surprised at Vicky's height; great interest is taken in her. We went on to a cottage (formerly Jean Gordon's) to visit old widow Simons, who is past four-score, with a nice rosy face, but was bent quite double; she was most friendly, shaking hands with us all, asking which was I, and repeating many kind blessings: 'May the Lord attend ye with mirth and with joy; may He ever be with ye in this world, and when ye leave it.' To

Vicky, when told she was going to be married, she said, 'May the Lord be a guide to ye in your future, and may every happiness attend ye.' She was very talkative; and when I said I hoped to see her again, she expressed an expectation that she should be called any day, and so did Kitty Kear.

"We went into three other cottages; to Mrs. Symon's (daughter-in-law to the old widow living next door), who had an unwell boy; then across a little burn to another old woman's; and afterwards peeped into Blair the fiddler's. We drove back, and got out again to visit old Mrs. Grant (Grant's mother), who is so tidy and clean, and to whom I gave a dress and handkerchief, and she said, 'You're too kind to me, you're over kind to me, ye give me more every year and I get older every year.' After talking some time with her, she said, 'I am glad to see ye looking so nice.'" She had tears in her eyes, and speaking of Vicky's going, said, 'I'm very sorry, and I think she is sorry hersel';' and having said she feared she would not see (the Princess) again, said, 'I am sorry I said that, but I meant no harm, I always say just what I think, not what is fut (fit).' Dear old lady; she is such a pleasant person.

"Really the affection of these good people, who are so hearty and so happy to see you, taking interest in everything, is very touching and gratifying."

CHAPTER XVII.

THE FIRST WEDDING IN OUR ROYAL FAMILY.

PRINCE FREDERICK WILLIAM OF PRUSSIA'S PROPOSAL TO THE PRINCESS ROYAL—THEIR ENGAGEMENT—CONFIRMATION OF THE PRINCESS—HER SERIOUS ACCIDENT—THE QUEEN'S SPEECH TO THE OFFICERS AND SOLDIERS FROM THE CRIMEA—THE WEDDING—THE DEPARTURE OF THE PRINCESS FOR HER NEW HOME.

THE first marriage in a family is always of great importance, making, as it often does, the first break in the home circle. The Princess Royal was only fifteen years of age, when the Prince of Prussia, the heir of the childless King, proposed for her in marriage in the name of the Prince's only son, Prince Frederick William, a young man of twenty-four and nearly ten years the senior of the Princess Royal. From the Queen's friendship with the Prince and Princess of Prussia, their son was well known and much liked in the English Royal Family, and the youthful Princess was favourably inclined towards him. The proposal was graciously received, but, as the young Princess had not even been confirmed, it was decided that the young couple must become better acquainted

M

and that nothing must be said to the Princess until after her confirmation. But, eventually, the Prince paid a delightfully private visit to the Royal family in their Highland retreat, and then he was allowed to plead his cause under the happiest circumstances.

The Queen thus mentions the matter in her book,

September 29, 1855.

"Our dear Victoria was this day engaged to Prince Frederick William of Prussia, who had been on a visit to us since the 14th. He had already spoken to us, on the 20th, of his wishes; but we were uncertain, on account of her extreme youth, whether he should speak to her himself, or wait till he came back again. However, we felt that it was better he should do so, and during our ride up *Craig-na-Ban* this afternoon, he picked a piece of white heather, (the emblem of 'good luck,') which he gave to her; and this enabled him to make an allusion to his hopes and wishes, as they rode down *Glen Girnoch*, which led to this happy conclusion."

The Prince Consort mentioned the young lovers in his half-tender, half-humourous way, to his friend Baron Stockmar, saying how 'the young man' was really in love, 'the young lady' doing her best to please him.

The confirmation of the Princess took place on the 20th of the following March in the private Chapel at

Windsor. The Archbishop of Canterbury and the Bishop of London officiated, in the presence of the Queen and Royal family, the Ministers, officers of State, &c. Prince Albert led in the Princess, while her Godfather, King Leopold, followed with the Queen. Bishop Wilberforce briefly made a note of the scene in the following words, "To Windsor Castle. The Confirmation of Princess Royal. Interesting. She devout, composed, earnest. Younger sister much affected. The Queen and Prince also."

In June a serious accident, which might have been fatal, occurred to the Princess Royal, while Prince Frederick William was on a visit in England, as he frequently appears to have been. The young Princess was sealing a letter when the sleeve of her muslin dress caught fire and blazed up instantly. Happily the Princesses' governess, Miss Hildyard, and the Princess Alice, who was receiving a lesson from her music-mistress, were in the room, and they succeeded in putting out the fire by wrapping the hearthrug round the Princess. By their presence of mind her life was probably saved. The arm was burnt rather badly but not so as to be permanently disfigured. Lady Bloomfield, after relating how the Princess was, 'quite charming. Her manners were so perfectly unaffected and unconstrained, and she was so full of fun,' goes on to say, 'when she, the Princess, burnt her arm she never uttered a cry, she said, "Don't frighten Mamma—send for Papa, first." Afterwards, she wrote to her music-mistress, dictating the letter and signing it with her left hand lest the lady, who had been present when the accident occurred, would be anxious. In passing, we must just mention one little scene which occurred soon afterwards in July. The Queen and the Prince were at Aldershot for the Review of the troops which had returned from the Crimea. The weather was unfortunately very wet, but, during a short break in the rain, the Crimean regiments formed three sides of a square round the carriage in which the Queen sat. *"The officers and four men of each of the troops that had been under fire 'stepped out' and the Queen, standing up in the carriage, addressed them.

"'Officers, non-commissioned officers, and soldiers, I wish personally to convey through you to the regiments assembled here this day my hearty welcome on their return to England in health and full efficiency. Say to them that I have watched anxiously over the difficulties and hardships which they have so nobly borne, that I have mourned with deep sorrow for the brave men who have fallen in their country's cause, and that I have felt proud of that valour which, with their gallant allies, they have displayed on every field. I thank God that your dangers are over, while the glory

---

* "Queen Victoria.," by Miss Tytler.

of your deeds remains; but I know that, should your services be again required, you will be animated with the same devotion which in the Crimea has rendered you invincible.'

"When the clear, sweet voice was silent, a cry of 'God save the Queen!' sprang to every lip. Helmets, bearskins, and shakos were thrown into the air; the dragoons waved their sabres, and a shout of loyal acclamation, caught up from line to line, rang through the ranks.

"The next day, in Summer sunshine, the Queen and the City of London welcomed home the Guards. In anticipation," Miss Tytler says, "of a brilliant review in the Park, she saw them march past from the central balcony of Buckingham Palace, as she had seen them depart on the chill February morning more than two years before; another season and another scene — not unchastened in its triumph, for many a once familiar face was absent, and many a yearning thought wandered to Russian hill and plain and Turkish graveyard, where English sleepers rested till the great awakening."

One more incident we must relate before we return to the romance of the two young Royal lovers. Among the visitors at Balmoral in 1858, was Florence Nightingale. The Queen had before this given her a jewel in remembrance of her services in the Crimea. The design was this, "a field of white enamel was charged with a St. George's cross in ruby red enamel, from which shot rays of gold. This field was encircled by a black band bearing the scroll "Blessed are the merciful." The shield was set in a framework of palm-branches in green enamel tipped with gold, and united at the bottom by a riband of blue enamel inscribed 'CRIMEA' in gold letters. The cypher V. R. surmounted by a crown in diamonds, was charged upon the centre of the cross. On the back was a gold tablet which bore an inscription from the hand of Her Majesty."

But, to return to the Princess Royal, the Prince Consort, feeling certain that his eldest daughter would have to depend largely upon her own qualities to conciliate the affection of the German people sought, with loving earnestness, to prepare her for the task. He superintended special studies designed to give her a grasp of political knowledge and to fit her to take part in what was destined to be her public life. And, we doubt not, that, in that, both father and daughter possessed the Queen's true, intelligent sympathy. But the mother wrote concerning the Princess Royal's last days at Balmoral:—

"Vicky suffers under the feeling that every spot she visits she has to greet for the last time as *home*. As I look on, the "*Johanna sagt euch Lebewohl!* of the "Maid of Orleans" comes frequently into my mind.

It has been my lot to go through the same experiences."

On the day before the Court left Windsor Castle for the wedding at St. James's Palace, the Queen's Diary has the following entry:—

"Went to look at the rooms prepared for Vicky's honeymoon, very pretty. It quite agitated me to see them......... Poor, poor child! We took a short walk with Vicky, who was dreadfully upset at this real break in her life—the real separation from her childhood."

On the 25th of January, 1858, the Queen writes:—

"The second most eventful day in my life as regards feelings. I felt as if I were being married over again myself, only much more nervous, for I had not that blessed feeling which I had then, which raises and supports one, of giving myself up for life to him whom I loved and worshipped—then and ever............ Got up, and while dressing, dearest Vicky came to see me, looking well and composed, and in a fine quiet frame of mind. She had slept more soundly and better than ever. This relieved me greatly........."

The marriage went off under the brightest auspices. The Queen was excited, but deeply impressed with the pageant, while the Royal group was being photographed. "I trembled so, my likeness has come out indistinct," she wrote, and, "The effect was very solemn and impressive as we passed through the rooms, down the staircase, and across a covered-in court."

"Then came the Bride's procession and our darling Flower looked very touching and lovely, with such an innocent, confident and serious expression, her veil hanging back over her shoulders, walking between her beloved father and dearest Uncle Leopold, who had been at her christening and confirmation, and was himself the widower of Princess Charlotte, heiress to the throne of this country. Albert's and my uncle, Mamma's brother, one of the wisest kings in Europe. My last fear of being overcome vanished on seeing Vicky's quiet, calm and composed manner. It was beautiful to see her kneeling with Fritz, their hands joined and the train borne by the eight young ladies, who looked like a cloud of maidens hovering round her as they knelt near her. Dearest Albert took her by the hand to give her away. My beloved Albert (who, I saw, felt so strongly,) which reminded me vividly of having in the same way proudly, tenderly, confidently, most lovingly knelt by him on this very same spot, and having our hands joined there."

The Prince's feelings are not less tenderly recorded. "I do not trust myself to speak of Tuesday," he writes, "on which day we are to lose her," the day which the Queen said "hangs like a cloud above us."

On the Sunday, the day after the bridegroom arrived,

the Princess Royal gave her mother a brooch, with her own hair in it, clasping her in her arms and telling her that she "hoped to be worthy to be her child."

That was before the service at which Canon Wilberforce preached an eloquent sermon.

There was a beautiful wedding, and, a few days after it, came the last Sunday before the dreaded separation, which was made so much more formidable by the knowledge that, owing to the many duties which would devolve upon her, the Princess would not be able often nor for long, to return to the home which she was now leaving.

The Queen wrote reverently on that day, "But God will carry us through, as He did on the 25th, and we have the comfort of seeing the dear young people so perfectly happy."

On Monday the Queen felt very unhappy about it, and the Princess Royal confided to her mother that she thought it would kill her to take leave of her father.

Tuesday, the 2nd of February, was dark and cold with snow beginning to fall, unpropitious weather apparently for a long journey unless there is truth in the Scotch saying, which declares a bride to be happy who goes "a white gate" (Road).

The Royal mother wrote, "I clasped her in my arms and blessed her. I kissed good Fritz, and pressed his hand again and again. He was unable to speak, and the tears were in his eyes."

The Prince Consort and the Prince of Wales accompanied the bride and bridegroom to Gravesend.

We are told, "The Londoners assembled in crowds to see the last of their Princess on her route to the coast by the Strand, Cheap and London Bridge. Many persons recall to this day the sorrowful scene in the cheerless snowy weather. This was the reverse side of all the splendid wedding festivities, the bride of seventeen quitting family, home and native country, sitting grave and sad beside her equally pale and silent father, the couple so tenderly attached, on the eve of the final parting. At Gravesend, where young girls, in spite of the snow, strewed flowers before the bride's steps, the Prince waited to see the ship sail—not without risk in the snowstorm—for Antwerp. But no daughter appeared for a last look, the passionate sorrow of youth hid itself from view."

Afterwards, the Princess wrote almost every day "sometimes twice a day" to her mother, and regularly once a week to her father.

But, at home, the blank which was caused by her absence was great, until gradually the Princess Alice filled more and more the elder sister's vacant place.

CHAPTER XVIII.

GLAD SCENES AND SORROWFUL.

THE PRINCE CONSORT AND QUEEN ON THEIR WAY TO VISIT THE PRINCESS ROYAL—DEATH OF "CARL" A TRUSTED VALET—THE JOYFUL MEETING—GLIMPSES OF PRINCESS BEATRICE AND OF PRINCESS ALICE—DEATH OF THE DUCHESS OF KENT.

IN August Her Majesty and the Prince Consort went to pay a visit to their daughter in her German home. We can imagine the joy of the anticipated meeting. During a halt at Dusseldorf, however, Prince Albert received a telegram announcing the death of his faithful valet, Carl, who had been in his service ever since the Prince was a child of eight. It was a severe blow to both the Prince and Queen.

"While I was dressing," wrote the Queen, "Albert came in quite pale, with a telegram, saying, 'My poor Carl is dead' (Carl had been Prince Albert's valet for twenty-nine years). I turn sick now (14th August) in writing it......... 'He died suddenly on Saturday at Morges.' I burst into tears. All day the tears would rush every moment to my eyes, and this dreadful reality came to throw a gloom over the long-wished-for day of meeting with our dear child. Carl was with Albert from his seventh year. He was invaluable; well-educated, thoroughly trustworthy, devoted to the Prince, the best of nurses, superior in every sense of the word, a proud independent Swiss, who was quite *un homme de confiance*, peculiar but extremely careful, and who might be trusted in everything. He wrote well and copied much for us. He was the only link my loved one had about him which connected him with his childhood, the only one with whom he could talk over old times. I cannot think of my dear husband without Carl! He seemed part of himself. We were so thankful for and proud of this old servant; he was such a comfort to us, and now he has gone. A sad breakfast we had indeed, Albert felt the loss so much, and we had to choke our grief down all day."

It was no day for sorrow, yet the Queen and Prince mourned thus for their faithful servant.

Soon, afterwards, the train which bore the Royal parents towards their much-loved daughter passed the station at Rückeburg, where stood the aged Baroness Bunsen, the Queen's good old governess, waving her handkerchief.

And, at last, at Magdeburg, Prince Frederick William appeared, "radiant," with the welcome intelligence, that his Princess was at the Wildpark Station.

The Queen wrote, "There on the platform stood our darling child, with a nosegay in her hand. She stepped in, and long and warm was the embrace as she clasped me in her arms; so much to say and to tell and to ask, yet so unaltered; looking well, quite the old Vicky still. It was a happy moment for which I thank God."

Her Majesty stayed at the Palace of Babelsburg during her visit which lasted more than a fortnight. In addition to being once more with their daughter, the Prince and Queen became acquainted with that daughter's surroundings. Henceforward they would be able to imagine more correctly what she was doing and where she would be.

Much good counsel had the Prince given his daughter upon her entrance on the new duties and responsibilities of her life, and it must have been very gratifying to both him and the Queen to find how ably the Princess was carrying out these manifold instructions.

A good anecdote is told of her Royal Highness when she first went to live at Berlin. It seems a Prussian Princess is not allowed by her mistress of the robes to take up a chair, carry it across the whole breadth of the room and put it down at the other side. Countess Perponcher, we are told, discovered the Princess

Royal performing such an act and earnestly remonstrated with her.

Upon which the Princess said,—

"I'll tell you what, my dear Countess; you are probably aware of the fact of my mother being the Queen of England?"

The Countess bowed.

"Well," continued the Princess, "then I must reveal to you another fact; Her Majesty, the Queen of Great Britain and Ireland has not once, but very often, so far forgotten herself as to take up a chair. I speak from personal observation, I can assure you. Nay, if I am not greatly deceived, I noticed one day my mother carrying a chair in each hand, in order to set them for her children. Do you really think that my dignity forbids anything which is frequently done by the Queen of England?"

The Countess bowed again and retired, doubtless not a little surprised at the information she had received.

But to return to the visit of the Prince and Queen, it was, we are told, a pleasant one, Her Majesty attended two great reviews, and gave a day to the Berlin Museum.

The Prince Consort's birthday was celebrated while he and the Queen were staying at his daughter's house.

And then, with tears and a brave "*Auf baldiges*

wiedersehn" (to a speedy meeting again), the Royal party separated.

Later, when the Princess Royal became a mother and our Queen a grandmother, we have an amusing glimpse of the little Princess Beatrice. Her father wrote to his eldest daughter,

"The little girl must be a darling. Little girls are much prettier than boys. I advise her to model herself after her aunt Beatrice. That excellent lady has now not a moment to spare. 'I have no time,' she says, 'to do anything, I must write letters to my niece.'"

In April 1859, the Princess Alice was confirmed. The Queen wrote, "She is very good, gentle, sensible and amiable, and a real comfort to me." And we are told, "Without her sister, the Princess Royal's remarkable intellectual power, Princess Alice had fine intelligence. She was also fair to see in her Royal maidenhood."

In 1859, she visited Coburg again with her parents, where once more they had the pleasure of meeting the Princess Royal with her little son. The visit was saddened by the death of Prince Albert's step-mother, the Duchess-Dowager of Coburg just before the arrival of the Prince and Queen. And, before their return, the Prince had, again, what might have been a serious accident.

In December the Princess Alice was betrothed to the Prince Louis of Hesse.*

In March of the next year Her Majesty had the inexpressible grief of losing her mother, the Duchess of Kent.

Space will not permit us to linger here upon the touching scene which we have elsewhere described at some length. Her Majesty herself permits her loyal subjects to witness something of her sorrow, as she wrote, that when the end was approaching,—

"I knelt before her, (the Duchess of Kent) kissed her dear hand, and placed it next my cheek; but though she opened her eyes she did not I think know me. She brushed my hand off, and the dreadful reality was before me that for the first time she did not know the child she had ever received with such tender smiles. I went out to sob......... I asked the doctors if there was no hope; they said they feared none whatever, for consciousness had left her."

The long night passed in sorrowful watching. In the morning, the Prince took the Queen from the room, and when she returned the windows and doors were thrown open. Her Majesty sat down on a footstool and held her mother's hand, while the paleness of death stole over the face, and the features grew longer and sharper.

See "Scenes in the Life of the Princess Alice."

Albert Memorial and Hall, South Kensington.

"I fell on my knees," wrote the Queen, afterwards, "holding the beloved hand which was still warm and soft, though heavier, in both of mine. I felt the end was fast approaching, as Clark went out to call Albert and Alice, I only left gazing on that beloved face, and feeling as if my heart would break......... It was a solemn, sacred, never to be forgotten scene. Fainter and fainter grew the breathing, at last it ceased but there was no change of countenance, nothing; the eyes closed as they had been for the last half-hour. The clock struck half-past nine at the very moment. Convulsed with sobs I fell on the hand and covered it with kisses. Albert lifted me up and took me into the next room, himself entirely melted into tears, which is unusual for him, deep as his feelings are, and clasped me in his arms. I asked if all was over; he said 'Yes.'"

Years afterwards the Princess Alice remembered how her father took her to her mother with the words, "Comfort Mamma," and nobly was the command obeyed not only then, but later, when that dear husband and father was himself the object of their deep mourning.

The moment the Princess Royal heard of the death, we are told, she started for England, and arrived there two days afterwards.

The Duchess of Kent by her will bequeathed her

property to the Queen and appointed the Prince Consort her sole executor.

"He was so tender and kind," Her Majesty wrote, "so pained to have to ask me distressing questions, but spared me so much. Everything done so quickly and feelingly."

CHAPTER XIX.

THE DEATH OF THE PRINCE CONSORT.

THE PRINCE CONSORT'S LETTER TO THE DUCHESS OF KENT ON THE ANNIVERSARY OF HIS WEDDING DAY—LAST EVENTS OF HIS LIFE—HIS ILLNESS—DEATH—FUNERAL—WORDS OF THE POET LAUREATE.

RATHER more than a month before the Duchess of Kent's death, the Prince Consort had written to her on the occasion of the 21st anniversary of his and the Queen's wedding-day:—

"Buckingham Palace, Feb. 10th, 1861.

"—I cannot let this day go by without writing to you, even if I had not to thank you for your kind wishes and the charming photographs. Twenty-one years make a good long while, and to-day our marriage 'comes of age, according to law.' We have faithfully kept our pledge for better and for worse, and have only to thank God that He has vouchsafed so much happiness to us. May He have us in His keeping for the days to come! You have, I trust, found good and loving children in us, and we have experienced nothing but love and kindness from you. In the hope that your pains and aches will now leave you soon, — I remain, as ever, your affectionate son,

"Albert."

How little the Prince could have known that the happy married life of which he spoke, should be, as regards this world, so nearly at an end. Yet he was often far from well during that last year of his life, and when his mother-in-law left him her sole executor this greatly increased his labours. For he had to examine her papers and correspondence and adjust the claims of relations and retainers. And, all the time, he had to comfort and support Her Majesty in her natural grief at this first great family bereavement.

Much sympathy was felt for the Queen by all the country, and great respect was manifested for the life and character of the Duchess of Kent.

People remembered, then, how in those old days now so long past, the young widow had most self-sacrificingly chosen to stay in what to her was a foreign country, for the sake of her child and of that nation over whom that child was in all probability destined to reign.

Death, and the love and sympathy with which the actions of the dead are often regarded, sets things in a clearer light, and makes people recognise many things which before were hidden from their eyes. And so the Houses of Parliament, and the nation generally, showed their esteem for the memory of the noble Duchess, who had lived such a long and useful life.

In the retirement of Osborne, the Queen mourned for her mother with tender fidelity.

In August, Her Majesty and the Prince, accompanied by Prince Alfred (who was just home from the West Indies) and the Princesses Alice and Helena, paid another visit to Ireland. The Prince of Wales was already there, serving in the Curragh Camp, and the royal party attended a field day at the Curragh.

Afterwards the Lakes of Killarney were visited, which Her Majesty greatly enjoyed, naming, we are told, a point in the course of a row on one of the lakes.

The Prince Consort was much delighted with the beautiful and grand scenery.

"This is perfectly sublime," he said, again and again. His last birthday was spent in Ireland. The Queen wrote:—

"This is the dearest of days, and one which fills my heart with love, and gratitude and emotion. God bless and protect for ever my beloved Albert, the best and purest of human beings."

The day was kept quietly, all regretting the absence of the children 'above all, baby,' and the blank which was occasioned by the death of the childrens' kind grandmother.

From Ireland they went to Balmoral, where they had fine weather and much happiness. The Prince was able to enjoy his favourite recreation of deer-stalking, and Her Majesty to enjoy the scenery and the air.*

The Royal Party was at Windsor Castle again in October, and in November, the Queen wrote:—

"This was our dear Bertie's twentieth birthday. I pray God to assist our efforts to make him turn out well."

A few days afterwards Her Majesty became very anxious about her husband's failing health. Family trouble, too, had been distressing both the Prince and Queen. The Princess Royal was not well, and the King of Portugal, to whom they were both much attached had died of fever.

On the 19th, the Prince wrote almost his last letter to his eldest daughter, on her twenty-first birthday.

"May your life," he said, "which has begun beautifully, expand still further to the good of others and the contentment of your own mind! True inward happiness is to be sought only in the internal consciousness of effort systematically directed to good and useful ends. Success, indeed, depends upon the blessing which the most High sees fit to vouchsafe to our endeavours. May this success not fail you, and may your outward

---

* For a further account of this visit see "Scenes in the Life of the Princess Alice."

life leave you unhurt by the storms to which the sad heart so often looks forward with a shrinking dread."

On Sunday the first of December, Prince Albert walked out on the terrace, and attended chapel with the rest of his family, but was really very ill.

Low fever was next apprehended, and Dr. Jenner began to attend him. But on the fifth it was thought the Prince was rather better. He took a little nourishment with some relish and listened to the Princess Alice reading aloud.

Her Majesty wrote,—

"I found my Albert most dear and affectionate, and quite himself when I went in with little Beatrice, whom he kissed. He quite laughed at some of her new French verses, which I made her repeat; then he held her little hand in his for some time, and she stood looking at him. He then soon dozed off, having done so a great deal through the day, and I left, not to disturb him."

The Prince had long resisted the wish of his medical attendants that he should undress and go to bed, but, at last, he yielded to their entreaties. At his own request he was moved on the 8th of December to a larger room, which happened to be the one in which both William IV. and George IV. had died.

Some of the entries in the Queen's Diary are very

touching. She had constantly to leave her husband to attend to the demands of the State, which now she had to meet alone, and it must have been the greatest comfort to her to know that when she was absent the Princess Alice was his devoted companion and nurse. The Princess would read to him, play and sing for him, and to her he could speak freely of those things respecting his danger to which the Queen could, naturally, not bear to listen just then. Yet, we are told, he would brighten up when Her Majesty approached.

"He was so kind, calling me *gutes Weibchen* (good little wife) and liking me to hold his dear hand," wrote the Queen, "Oh, it is an anxious, anxious time, but God will help us through it."

And again,

"Another good night for which I thank God. I went over at eight and found Albert taking his beef-tea. I supported him, and he laid his dear head, (his beautiful face, more beautiful than ever, has grown so thin) on my shoulder, and remained a little while saying, 'It is very comfortable so, dear child,' which made me so happy."

He would sometimes tenderly caress the Queen calling her in German, "Dear little wife, good little wife."

Once, as he was being assisted from his bed to the sofa, he said, as he stopped to look at a copy on porcelain of the Madonna and child by Raphael;—

"It helps me through half the day."

We are told that at the beginning of his illness, one of his physicians said, "Your Royal Highness will be better in a few days."

But he replied, "No, I shall not recover, but I am not taken by surprise. I am not afraid. I trust I am prepared."

The last sermon the Prince had heard at Balmoral was preached by the Rev. — Stewart, of St. Andrews, from the text, "Prepare to meet thy God," and the Prince had been so much interested in it that he had asked to see the manuscript.

On the last Sunday of his life, as Princess Alice, who had been playing several of his favourite chorals for him while the rest of the family were in Church asked, —" Were you asleep, dear Papa," as he was lying back with shut eyes and hands folded as if in prayer.

"Oh, no," he replied, "only I have such sweet thoughts."

The last day of his precious life came all too soon, and when Her Majesty went into his room, she found him "gazing as it were on unseen objects, and not taking notice of me."

The day being fine and bright, and the Queen being terribly overwhelmed with trouble, she asked if she might go out for a breath of air. To which the doctors replied, "Yes, just for a quarter of an hour."

And so Her Majesty went on the terrace with the Princess Alice, but hearing the Military Band, to which they had so often listened together in happier hours, playing at some distance, it was too much for her, and, bursting into tears, she went in again.

Some hours passed without much change except that an ominous dusky hue stole over the features of the beloved Prince. Then, he, who had always been so prompt and energetic, folded his arms and arranged his hair as he used to do when he was dressing, and, as if he were preparing, said the Queen, "for another and greater journey."

His last loving words were addressed to Her Majesty. He said in German, "Good little wife," kissed her and with a moaning sigh, laid his head upon her shoulder.

And not long before the end came, the Queen bent over her husband, saying in German "It is your little wife."

The dying Prince, recognising her voice, bowed his head and kissed her. Her Majesty retired into another room to weep, but was soon fetched back again. She knelt by her husband's side holding his hand, six of their children knelt around, the Duke of Cambridge and other gentlemen of the Court were present.

"The Castle clock chimed the third quarter after ten," wrote Sir Theodore Martin, "calm and peaceful grew the beloved form; the features settled into the beauty of a perfectly serene repose; two or three long but gentle sighs were drawn, and that great soul had fled, to seek a nobler scope for its aspirations in the world within the veil, for which it had often yearned, where there is rest for the weary, and where the spirits of the just are made perfect."

Shortly after midnight the great bell of St. Paul's proclaimed the Prince's death far and wide.

Terrible was the distress of the Royal Family. For three days the Queen was utterly prostrate with grief. The Princess Alice wrote years afterwards of that dreadful time, wondering how she and her mother could possibly have survived it.

The news of her father's death had to be communicated to the Princess Royal at Berlin, and to the young Prince Leopold at Cannes. The latter was in great grief over the death of his guardian, General Bowater, who had just expired in the room next to his Royal Highness, when the telegram arrived announcing the death of the Prince Consort. When it was opened it was found to contain the words, "Prince Albert is dead."

Prince Leopold's grief knew no bounds, and he cried in his desolation;—

"My mother, I must go to my mother......... My mother will bring him back again. Oh! I want my mother."

With the greatest difficulty the Queen had been prevailed upon to leave the fever-tainted air for Osborne. It was only when the plea was urged that it was for her children's sake that Her Majesty yielded, and, after visiting Frogmore, where she chose a site for the Prince's Mausoleum, she sought the retirement which was to be found there, in her grief and loneliness.

The Prince of Wales was the chief mourner at the funeral, which took place on the 23rd of December, and he was supported by his brother, Prince Arthur. The Royal children and officers of State were filled with grief.

One of the Prince Consort's favourite chorales was sung at his grave;—

> "I shall not in the grave remain,
>   Since Thou death's bond hast severed;
> But hope with Thee to rise again,
>   From fear of death delivered.
> I'll come to Thee, where'er Thou art—
> Live with Thee, from Thee never part;
>   Therefore to die is rapture.

> "And so to Jesus Christ I'll go,
>   My longing and extending;
> So fall asleep in slumbering deep—
>   Slumber that knows no ending—

> Till Jesus Christ, God's only Son,
> Opens the gates of bliss—leads on
> To Heaven—to life eternal!"

Inscribed upon the Prince's coffin were the words;—

"Here lies the most illustrious and exalted Albert, Prince Consort, Duke of Saxony, Prince of Saxe-Coburg and Gotha, Knight of the Most Noble Order of the Garter, the most beloved husband of the most august and potent Queen Victoria.

"He died on the 14th day of December 1861, in the forty-third year of his age."

The universal mourning and evidences of the nation's sorrow showed that, though Prince Albert had been sometimes misunderstood, yet that now, at last justice was done to his memory.

The Poet Laureate's words found their echo in many a heart when he said,

> "And indeed he seems to me
> Scarce other than my own ideal knight,
> Who reverenced his conscience as his king;
> Whose glory was redressing human wrong;
> Who spake no slander, no, nor listen'd to it;
> Who loved one only, and who clave to her—
> Her—over all whose realms, to their last isle,
> Commingled with the gloom of imminent war,
> The shadow of his loss drew like eclipse,
> Darkening the world. We have lost him: he is gone.

We know him now: all narrow jealousies
Are silent; and we see him as he moved,
How modest, kindly, all-accomplished, wise,

* * * * *

.........thro' all this tract of years
Wearing the white flower of a blameless life,
Before a thousand peering littlenesses,
In that fierce light which beats upon a throne,
And blackens every blot........"

CHAPTER XX.

MARRIAGES IN THE ROYAL FAMILY.

THE QUEEN'S SYMPATHY WITH THE SUFFERERS FROM THE HARTLEY COLLIERY ACCIDENT—DR. MACLEOD—MARRIAGE OF PRINCESS ALICE AND PRINCE LOUIS OF HESSE—PRESENTATION OF A BIBLE FROM THE WIDOWS OF ENGLAND TO THE QUEEN—THE PRINCE OF WALES'S MARRIAGE—THE PRINCESS OF WALES.

THE Queen spent most of the next year in retirement. Princess Alice was made the great medium of communication between Her Majesty and her Ministers. But that the Queen was not unmindful of the sorrows of her people was evident. The year had scarcely begun before a fearful accident occurred in the Hartley Colliery, near Newcastle-on-Tyne. An immense iron beam, connected with the pumping apparatus broke, and there was a terrible crash; the whole of the stages, props, gearing and everything between the mouth of the pit and the bottom gave way, and the two hundred and five men who were in the colliery were buried alive. Men and boys worked with all their power, encouraged by sounds from below, but a week elapsed before they were able to reach the buried men, who, unfortunately by that time had all expired. Touching memorandums of how they had passed their last days were found, together with messages to friends and relatives, scratched on flasks, boxes, and anything upon which it had been possible to write. The same hymn, "Rock of Ages," which had comforted their dying Prince, had been sung by these poor colliers, and then they had laid quietly down in rows to die.

The Queen sent the following message to the poor suffering wives and children who had thus terribly lost their guardians and bread-winners:—

"Her Majesty's tenderest sympathy is with the poor widows and mothers, and her own misery only makes her feel the more for them. Her Majesty hopes that everything will be done, as far as possible, to alleviate their distress, and Her Majesty will have the sad satisfaction in assisting in such a measure."

Many followed the Queen's example, and a subscription, for the relief of the sufferers was set on foot, which reached £81,000.

When Her Majesty went to Scotland for the first time after the death of the Prince Consort, she requested that Dr. Macleod might be in attendance. And her birthday was spent there. Dr. Macleod thus wrote of what he felt and experienced on that occasion:—

"I am never tempted to conceal any conviction from the Queen, for I feel she sympathises with what is

THE ROYAL MAUSOLEUM, FROGMORE.

true, and likes the speaker to utter the truth exactly as he believes it.......... All has passed well, that is to say, God enabled me to speak in private and in public to the Queen in such a way as seemed to me to be truth, the truth in God's sight, that which I believed she needed, though I feel it would be very trying to receive it. And what fills me with deepest thanksgiving is that she has received it, and has written to me such a kind, tender letter of thanks for it, which shall be treasured in my heart while I live.

"After dinner I was summoned unexpectedly to the Queen's room. She was alone. She met me, and, with an unutterably sad expression, which filled my eyes with tears, at once began to speak to me about the Prince. It is impossible for me to recall distinctly the sequence or substance of that long conversation. She spoke of his excellencies, his love, his cheerfulness, how he was everything to her. She said she never shut her eyes to trials, but liked to look them in the face; how she would never shrink from duty, but that all was at present done mechanically; that her highest ideas of purity and love were obtained from him, and that God could not be displeased with her love. But there was nothing morbid in her grief. I spoke freely to her about all I felt regarding him— the love of the nation and their sympathy—and took every opportunity of bringing before her the reality of

God's love and sympathy, her noble calling as a Queen, the value of her life to the nation, the blessedness of prayer."

The Princess Alice, whose marriage had been delayed by her father's death, was married very quietly, on the 1st of July, to Prince Louis of Hesse. The Prince of Wales returned from his tour in the East in time to be present. The young couple left England for Germany in about a week after the wedding. The Princess Alice was much beloved by the nation who did not forget what a comfort and support she had been in the hour of need. And many prayers and blessings followed her to her new home.

Her Majesty and the Royal family went abroad on the Continent in September, and it was then that the preliminaries of a marriage were arranged between the Prince of Wales and the Princess Alexandra of Denmark.

On the 9th of November, the Prince completed his twenty-first year, and there were rejoicings in London and the Provinces in honour of His Royal Highness's attainment of his majority.

In one of the closing days of this year the Duchess of Sutherland presented to the Queen a sumptuously-bound Bible, the gift of 'loyal English widows.' Her Majesty returned the following beautiful letter expressing her thanks for this offering.

"My dearest Duchess,—I am deeply touched by the gift of a Bible 'from many widows,' and by the very kind and affectionate address which accompanied it...... Pray express to all these kind sister-widows the deep and heartfelt gratitude of their widowed Queen, who can never feel grateful enough for the universal sympathy she has received, and continues to receive, from her loyal and devoted subjects. But what she values far more is their appreciation of her adored and perfect husband. To her, the only sort of consolation she experiences is in the constant sense of his unseen presence, and the blessed thought of the eternal union hereafter, which will make the bitter anguish of the present appear as naught. That our Heavenly Father may impart to 'many widows' those sources of consolation and support, is their broken-hearted Queen's earnest prayer.

Believe me, ever yours most affectionately,

"VICTORIA."

On the 7th of March, London, and indeed England, was alive with pleasurable excitement. For the Princess Alexandra, 'Sea-king's daughter from over the sea,' arrived off Gravesend as the bride-elect of the heir to the British Crown. She was accompanied by her father, mother, brother and sister, and was met by the Prince of Wales at Gravesend who drove with her through the streets of London, amidst the cheers of an enthusiastic crowd.

The wedding took place in St. George's Chapel on the 10th of March 1862. The Queen, who was attended by the Hon. Mrs. Bruce, was present in the Royal closet, in her widows' weeds. She looked down from thence upon the bride and bridegroom but she took no part in the brilliant ceremonial. All the members of the Royal Family were present, including Prince and Princess Louis of Hesse, and the Crown Princess of Prussia leading her little son.

The Princess Alexandria, 'whose beauty touched all hearts,' was in her nineteenth year, and the Prince of Wales in his twenty-second year. The latter wore a full general's uniform, with the stars of the Garter and the Indian Order, and the ribbon and band of the Golden Fleece round his neck, and, over his uniform, the mantle of the Garter.

The bride wore a dress of white satin and Honiton lace, with a silver moiré train. She also wore the bridegroom's gift consisting of a necklace, earrings, and brooch of pearls and diamonds, a rivière of diamonds given by the Corporation of London and valued at £10,000, and an opal and diamond bracelet, given by the Queen, &c.

During the service Her Majesty was much affected.

And Dr. McLeod, who was an interested spectator, observed that all the English Princesses wept behind their bouquets on beholding their brother waiting for his bride alone, and without the support of the father who had gone.

After the service the bride and bridegroom returned to the Castle, where they were received at the grand entrance by the Queen.

After the marriage had been attested in the white room, the bride and bridegroom left Windsor for Osborne where they spent their honeymoon.

The rejoicings were kept up for some days, London and the large towns being brilliantly illuminated in the evenings. On the 10th the crowds in the city were so great to witness the illuminations that six persons were crushed or trodden to death, and this sad circumstance caused the Prince of Wales to write a very sympathising letter which he addressed to the Lord Mayor.

Marlborough House was chosen to be the town residence of the Prince and Princess of Wales, and Sandringham as their country house.

The Princess of Wales is so well known and so much beloved by the English people that it is almost superfluous to mention here her many estimable qualities. After her marriage Her Royal Highness quite took her place as one of the Queen's daughters, being called by them affectionately "Alex," or "dear Alex," as Princess Alice often called her in her letters.

The writer of 'Our Queen,' a book which is very deservedly popular in this year of our Queen's Jubilee says, speaking of the Princess of Wales:—

"Her kindness of heart has always caused her to know how to do the right thing at the right time; as, for instance—when she was at Cambridge with the Prince, an undergraduate spread his gown on the pathway for her to walk on, she, although puzzled and amazed by the very superfluous act of devotion, lifted her dress and put her foot on the gown, bowing her acknowledgments to the student; and again, when she was visiting Denmark, the crowd of people under her window kept waiting and increasing so that she did not know what to do, until a happy thought struck her to gratify the assemblage by holding her baby in her arms before them, that all might see."

And again;—

"The Guelph Herald related an interesting anecdote of the kindness of the Princess:—'Crossing the Hall of Marlborough House late one afternoon, a few days before Christmas, her Royal Highness observed a young girl of singularly delicate and refined appearance, waiting, and also standing, though evidently fatigued and faint. The Princess kindly told her to sit down, asked her errand, and discovered that she had brought home some little garments which had been ordered for the children, and which the Princess, who is much interested in sewing machines and understands their merits, had desired should be made for her. Prepossessed by the modest, intelligent appearance and gentle manners of the girl, her Royal Highness desired her to follow her to her room, which she did without the remotest idea who the beautiful condescending lady was. After an examination of the articles, the Princess asked who it was that had executed the work. The girl modestly confessed that she had herself done most of it. The Princess said it was done very nicely, and finally drew from her the simple facts of her condition; how she had an invalid mother whom she was obliged to leave all alone while she went to a shop to work; how the fashionable rage for machine sewing had suggested to her to become a finished operator, with the hope that at some future time she might own a machine of her own, and earn something more than bread for her poor sick mother. The Princess rang the bell, ordered a bottle of wine, some biscuits and oranges, to be packed and brought to her; meanwhile, she had asked the wondering girl where she lived, and taken down the address upon her tablets. She then gave her the delicacies, which had been put into a neat little basket, and told her to take them to her mother.

"On Christmas morning, into the clean apartment of

the invalid mother and her astonished and delighted daughter, was borne a handsome sewing-machine, with a slip of paper on which were the words—'A Christmas-gift from Alexandra.'"

CHAPTER XXI.

LATER SCENES.

THE MARQUIS OF LORNE—HIS MARRIAGE WITH THE PRINCESS LOUISE—STORY OF THE MARCHIONESS OF LORNE—SERIOUS ILLNESS OF THE PRINCE OF WALES—THE THANKSGIVING DAY—DEATH OF DR. MACLEOD—ATTEMPTS ON THE QUEEN'S LIFE—HER MAJESTY'S BRAVERY—PRINCESS BEATRICE—THE DUKE OF ALBANY'S MARRIAGE AND DEATH—THE QUEEN OPENING THE INDIAN AND COLONIAL EXHIBITION.

SPACE will not allow us here, to describe the scenes of all the Royal weddings which took place, one by one, as Her Majesty's sons and daughters left her for homes of their own. But the marriage of the Princess Louise, deeply interesting as it was to the people of England because the bridegroom was not a prince, must be, at least, mentioned.

In the Queen's book, " Leaves from the Journal of our Life in the Highlands," upon the occasion of the Prince Consort and Her Majesty visiting Inverary, on August 18th 1847, the latter thus mentions the little Marquis of Lorne, whose future marriage with one of her daughters she could by no means have foreseen.

"The pipers walked before the carriage, and the Highlanders on either side, as we approached the house.

Outside stood the Marquis of Lorne, just two years old, a dear, white fat, fair little fellow, with reddish hair, but very delicate features, like both his father and mother; he is such a merry and independent little child. He had a black velvet dress and jacket, with a 'sporran' scarf and Highland bonnet."

During Her Majesty's visit to Balmoral, in the Autumn of 1870, the Princess Louise became engaged to the Marquis of Lorne. The engagement was made during a walk from the Glassalt Shiel to the Dhu Loch.

The Queen wrote in her Journal,—

"We got home by seven. Louise, who returned some time after we did, told me that Lorne had spoken of his devotion to her, and proposed to her, and that she had accepted him, knowing I would approve. Though I was not unprepared for this result, I felt painfully the thought of losing her. But I naturally gave my consent, and I could only pray that she might be happy."

Dr. Macleod, who had known Lord Lorne for a long time, was able to tell the Queen that he had a very high opinion of him, and that "he had fine, noble, elevated feelings."

The marriage took place on the 21st of March, 1871. Her Majesty showed her sanction of it by going to it in person, and giving her daughter away herself, by a gesture, when the usual question "Who giveth this woman to be married to this man?" was asked.

Many eyes were dim with tears as they looked upon the bride and the Queen mother, we are told, as they passed in the royal carriage to the Chapel. The Princess looked at the people through a bower of orange blossoms, and very hearty were their prayers of "God bless her."

The whole Royal family was present at the wedding, even the two little boys of the Prince and Princess of Wales, Prince George of Wales and Prince Albert Victor, in their Highland kilt, scarf and sporran, upon whom their mother's eyes rested fondly as they marched in front of her.

The bride had a bright and happy face, but she spoke in low tones, as she said the words,—

"I, Princess Louise, take thee John Douglas Sutherland, Marquis of Lorne, &c."

Princess Louise was then twenty-three and Lord Lorne twenty-six years of age.

The Princess Louise has been like her sisters in showing great kindness to the poor, and has ever been ready, when called upon, to assist in philanthropical objects of all kinds.

An amusing story was told us the other day, but upon what authority it rests we can scarcely say, of Her Royal Highness during her visit to Canada. It seems that she was one day walking, without any attendants very near her, when she approached a cottage within which an old woman was very busy at her ironing-table.

The Princess, being thirsty, asked her if she would kindly get her a glass of water. But that the old woman somewhat shortly refused to do. "The spring was at a little distance," she said, "and she was busy ironing her old man's shirt, for he was going with her to see the 'Queen's child' on the morrow.'"

Doubtless considerably amused, the Princess suggested that she would iron the shirt if the old lady would fetch her some water from the spring.

This was agreed to, and when the old woman returned, the Princess handed over to her the nicely-ironed garment, telling her, at the same time, that she was the daughter of the Queen.

The old woman's astonishment may be better imagined than described—but she declared her old man should never wear that shirt, for she would always keep it as it was as a memento of the "Queen's child."

At the close of 1871, the whole nation was plunged into gloom by the illness of the Prince of Wales; and the excitement respecting the daily bulletins was very great. The Prince, who lay ill of Typhoid fever at Sandringham, was devotedly nursed by his wife and the Princess Alice, who was staying with them at the time. The Queen went to be with them for a few days on the 29th of November, but, after remaining for a short time, as the Prince seemed to be progressing favourably, she returned to Windsor. On the 8th, however, the beloved patient had such a severe relapse that Her Majesty and the Royal family were sent for to Sandringham. For days the Prince hovered between life and death. By the Queen's desire special prayers were used, on and after the 10th, in all Churches and Chapels of the Establishment.

Prayers were also offered in the Jewish Synagogues, and in Roman Catholic and Dissenting Chapels.

On the 14th, the anniversary of the Prince Consort's death, the crisis of the disease was safely passed, and the invalid fell into the much desired and refreshing sleep.

The Queen returned to Windsor on the 19th, and on the 26th, she wrote as follows to her people,—

"The Queen is very anxious to express her deep sense of the touching sympathy of the whole nation on the occasion of the alarming illness of her dear son, the Prince of Wales. The universal feeling shown by her people during those painful, terrible days, and the sympathy evinced by them with herself and her beloved daughter, the Princess of Wales, as well as the general joy at the improvement of the Prince of Wales's state, have made a deep and lasting impression on her heart, which can never be effaced. It was indeed nothing new to her, for the Queen had met with the same sympathy when, just ten years ago, a similar illness removed from her side the mainstay of her life, the best, wisest and kindest of husbands. The Queen wishes to express, at the same time, on the part of the Princess of Wales, her feelings of heartfelt gratitude, for she has been as deeply touched as the Queen by the great and universal manifestation of loyalty and sympathy. The Queen cannot conclude without expressing her hope that her faithful subjects will continue their prayers to God for the complete recovery of her dear son to health and strength."

It is said that no public sight throughout Her Majesty's reign, was more moving than her progress, with the Prince and Princess of Wales, to and from St. Paul's, on the 27th of February, which had been appointed as the Thanksgiving day for the Prince of Wales's recovery.

The decorated streets were packed with enormous masses of people, the cheering was continuous. Her Majesty wore white flowers in her bonnet and looked happy and content.

Amidst the cheers, were mingled cries of "God save the Queen!" and "God bless the Prince of Wales."

His Royal Highness insisted on continually lifting his hat in response to the congratulations.

The Lord Mayor and a deputation from the Common Council met the Royal party at Temple Bar. The City Sword was presented and returned, after which the Lord Mayor remounted and rode before the Queen to St. Paul's.

The sight in the Cathedral, where 13,000 persons were gathered, was most imposing.

The Queen, taking her son's arm, and with the Princess of Wales on her left, walked up the nave to the pew which had been specially prepared for the Royal party.

The service began with the *Te Deum*, and then there was a special form of Thanksgiving, which began as follows:—

"O Father of mercies, O God of all comfort, we thank Thee that Thou hast heard the prayers of this nation in the day of our trial; we praise and magnify Thy glorious name for that Thou hast raised Thy servant Albert Edward, Prince of Wales, from the bed of sickness."

The sermon preached by the Archbishop of Canterbury was from the words in Romans, "*Members one of another*."

Upon their return to Buckingham Palace, the Queen and the Prince of Wales appeared for a short time on the central balcony.

In the evening, London was brilliantly illuminated.

On the 16th of June in that year Her Majesty had a great loss in the death of Dr. Macleod. We have already given some account of the relation in which he stood to Her Majesty, as her spiritual adviser, we can only add that the Queen, writing of him, said:—

"His own faith was so strong, his heart so large, that all, high and low, weak and strong, the erring and the good, could alike find sympathy, help and consolation from him. How I loved to talk to him, to ask his advice, to speak to him of my sorrows, my anxieties! But, alas! how impossible I feel it to be to give any adequate idea of the character of this good and distinguished man."

Her Majesty wrote about having had a talk with him soon after the Prince Consort's death, she said,—

"We talked of dear Albert's illness, his readiness to go at all times, with which Dr. Macleod was much struck, and said what a beautiful state of mind he must always have been in, how unselfish, how ready to do whatever was necessary; and I exemplified this by describing his cheerfulness in giving up all he liked and enjoyed, and being just as cheerful when he changed to other circumstances, looking at the bright and interesting side of them; like, for instance, going from here to Windsor, and from Windsor to London, leaving his own dear home &c., and yet being always cheerful which was the reverse with me. He spoke of the blessing of living on with those who were gone on before. An old woman whom he knew, he said, had lost her husband and several of her children, and had many sorrows, and he asked her how she had been able to bear them, and she answered,—

"'Ah! when *he* went awa' it made a great hole, and all the others went through it.' And so it is, most touchingly and truly expressed, and so it will be ever with me!"

The Queen wrote, after Dr. Macleod's last visit to the Castle, with sad foreboding :—

"Saw and wished dear Dr. Macleod good-bye with real regret and anxiety............ When I wished him good-bye and shook hands with him, he said, "God bless your Majesty," and the tears were in his eyes. Only then did the thought suddenly flash upon me, as I closed the door of my room, that I might never see this dear friend again, and it nearly overcame me. But this thought passed, and never did I think that not quite three years after his spirit would be with the God and Saviour he loved and served so well."

In 1878, on the 14th of November, the seventeenth anniversary of the decease of the Prince Consort, the Queen was bereaved by death of her beloved second daughter, the Princess Alice, Grand Duchess of Hesse.

The whole Royal Family of Darmstadt with the exception of one Princess had been prostrated with diptheria; and, after losing one little daughter, the Grand Duchess herself succumbed to the fatal malady.

Perhaps there is nothing in literature more touching than the succession of telegrams, which the afflicted lady had daily dispatched to her mother, the Queen; they contained condensed such a tale of sorrow bravely borne, and of suppressed suffering as is happily rarely to be met with.

And then, at last, when the invalids Her Royal Highness had nursed so devotedly were recovering nicely, the beloved wife and mother was herself struck down.

As we have elsewhere recorded,[*] the striking incidents of the close of the life of the Princess so deservedly loved and so widely mourned for by both English and German people, we will briefly mention here, that, after murmuring in her sleep, "Four weeks—Marie (the little daughter who had died)—my father—" she passed into that deeper sleep which knows no earthly waking.

The sympathy with Her Majesty was wide-spread and was eloquently expressed by both peer and prelate, in the Houses of Parliament and in Cathedrals and Churches, and all England rang with the praises of the inestimable daughter, the devoted sister, the cherished wife and the beloved mother who had died at the comparatively early age of thirty-five.

---

[*] In our book "Scenes in the Life of the Princess Alice."

Her Majesty's courage is a note-worthy feature in her character, and it has, we grieve to say, been tested several times by attempts which have been made upon her life, mostly by persons of unsound mind.

One young man called Oxford fired a pistol at the Queen, as she was driving up Constitution hill with Prince Albert, not long before the Princess Royal was born. The Prince, hearing, turned his head towards whence the sound proceeded, and the Queen rose at the same moment, but her husband immediately pulled her down by his side. And, happily, Her Majesty was not hurt.

There seemed to be no doubt that Oxford was of unsound mind, and he was, accordingly, confined first in Bedlam and then Dartmoor. Finally after thirty-five years, he was sent abroad upon his promising never to return to England, and a few years ago, he was earning his living as a house-painter in Melbourne.

On one occasion when an attack was apprehended, the Queen, with her usual bravery and kind consideration for others, would not permit her ladies to accompany her on her afternoon drive. But she went out with the Prince Consort alone, and, when they returned, the news of the attack which had been made spread through the Palace. The Queen said to Miss Lidell :—

"I dare say, Georgy, you were surprised at not driving with me this afternoon; but the fact was, that as we returned from Church yesterday a man presented a pistol at the carriage window, which flashed in the pan. We were so taken by surprise that he had time to escape; so I knew what was hanging over me, and I was determined to expose no life but my own."

On one occasion, the Princess Beatrice, showed similar presence of mind, for when she was driving with her mother, she saw the threatened danger but, as it was happily averted, she did not mention the matter until they had reached home.

The Princess Beatrice, who was the last of all our Queen's daughters to leave the mother whose constant companion she had been for so long, is an artist of considerable ability, and an accomplished pianist and vocalist. Indeed not only does she sing songs, but she composes them. Her *Birthday Book* ornamented with flowers and artistic designs is well known. And she, too, has followed the example of her older sisters in being kind and good to the poor and sick. The Order of the Royal Red Cross was conferred on her, because of the help she had given in supplying articles of comfort to the sick and wounded soldiers who were serving in Egypt. She is the President of the Belgrave Hospital for children, and is much interested in the St. John's Ambulance Society. In Bazaars for charitable objects her work is often seen and eagerly purchased. She has been, besides, frequently her mother's almoner, and has often visited the poor people on her mother's different estates.

Princess Beatrice is the only member of the Royal Family who has been married in a parish Church; and there was less of state ceremony in her's than in that of any of the Royal marriages.

It was in Whippingham Church, in the Isle of Wight, that she was married to Prince Henry of Battenberg, the third son of Prince Alexander of Hesse-Darmstadt.

The Princess had not the trial of leaving her home, as had her older sisters, as it was arranged that she should still continue to live with Her Majesty.

In March 1884, the Queen and the Royal Family sustained a heavy loss in the death of Prince Leopold, the Duke of Albany, at Cannes.

This youngest son of our beloved Queen had always been delicate, and had often been a source of great anxiety to Her Majesty. He was perhaps, the most scholarly of all the Queen's sons and was exceedingly good and virtuous. He had become deservedly popular in England, and, by his many public appearances, and grateful and winning speeches, had gained golden opinions on all sides. He is said to have been more like his father than any of his brothers.

In his twenty-ninth year he married the Princess Helen, fourth daughter of the reigning Prince and Princess Waldeck Pyremont, an old Protestant family connected with several of the reigning dynasties of Europe. It is said that the Princess is a pleasant, merry, exceedingly good-tempered, and well-informed young lady.

The young people seem to have met at the little watering-place of Soden, in the Autumn of 1881, and there in all probability the Prince fell in love with his future bride. He was, as we have said, in his twenty-ninth year, and she was eight years younger when they were married on the 27th of April 1882.

In 1883, their little daughter received "the dear and hallowed name of Alice."

In March 1884, the Duke went to Cannes, to escape the trying Spring east winds, leaving the Duchess, who was only in a delicate state of health, behind him at Claremont. Appearing to be benefitted by his stay at Cannes, he was unusually well and in excellent spirits. But on the 27th, in ascending a stair at the Cercle Nautique, he slipped and fell, injuring his ailing knee rather severely. No danger was, however, apprehended, and, knowing the tidings would make his wife anxious, the Duke wrote to her with his own hand. During the following night, his physician, feeling uneasy, watched by his patient. The Prince slept soundly until two, when he was seized with convulsions, and, a few minutes afterwards, expired in the arms of his equerry, Captain Percival.

The Duchess of Albany, whose apprehensions had been aroused by the telegrams about the accident, was sitting with Princess Christian in the library of Claremont House, when Dr. Royle's fatal telegram was brought in. It was opened by the Princess, and the poor young Duchess, rightly imagining that something disastrous had happened, begged to know the worst.

Princess Christian replied that Prince Leopold was dead.

The Duchess was quite stricken and mute for some time, being unable to realise her bereavement. Her Majesty's first and constant thought on hearing the sad news was for the poor young widow at desolate Claremont. The members of the Royal family and the nation at large felt the most tender sympathy for her.

The Prince of Wales started for Cannes and accompanied his Royal brother's remains to England.

On the arrival of the melancholy cavalcade at Windsor, the Queen went with Princess Christian and Princess Beatrice to the railway station to meet the body of her beloved son.

The Prince was buried in the Royal vault in St.

George's Chapel, Windsor Castle, the Queen, Princesses, and other ladies, being present.

In all parts of the country respect and sympathy for the sorrow of the Royal family was evinced, and fervent prayers were offered for the poor young Royal widow. We are told that,

"Shortly after the Prince's death a second baby came to cheer the loneliness of the Duchess's life. And the news was received with universal relief and thankfulness."

One more glimpse at a brighter scene may be permitted us before we close this little volume.

It is the day of the opening of the Colonial and Indian Exhibition, a perfect May-day, with brilliant sunshine and a pleasant breeze. The Queen, who is accompanied by the Crown Princess of Germany, Prince and Princess Henry of Battenberg, and Prince and Princess Louise of Battenberg, drives to the main entrance of the Exhibition, where, on entering the Colonial Hall, Her Majesty is received by the Prince of Wales, as President of the Executive Committee, and other members of the Royal family. The chief executive Commissioners for the various Colonies and India are presented to the Queen by the Prince.

Preceded by a fanfare from the heralds, the brilliant procession goes through the Indian Hall and down the middle Indian Court, the sunshine gilding the assemblage with a touch of Oriental splendour, which is heightened by the long flowing robes of the foreign visitors, and the Indian attendants.

The Queen is attired in black silk, with a white ostrich feather in her bonnet, the Princess of Wales wears a costume of striped blue silk, and the Prince of Wales is in his Field-Marshal's uniform.

As the Queen passes down the line, she is saluted on all sides with great respect, the Indians bowing in Oriental fashion. Her Majesty smiles and bows in return.

When the procession reaches the Albert Hall, the Queen takes her place in front of the chair of State, with the Prince of Wales on her right, and other members of the Royal Family grouped around, while the great officers of State surround the throne.

The Laureate's Ode, composed for the occasion and set to music by Sir Arthur Sullivan, is then sung; and the Prince of Wales reads the address to Her Majesty which gives an outline of the events which led up to the opening of the Exhibition.

The Queen reads her own reply, and her beautiful voice, which seems as clear and strong as in her girlhood's days, is heard in every part of the building.

After observing that she has received the addresses with the greatest satisfaction, Her Majesty goes on to say, she has watched with a warm and growing interest the progress of their proceedings, and it is gratifying to her to witness the successful result of their judicious and unremitting exertions in that magnificent Exhibition. She has been deeply moved by their reference to the exhibition of 1851, and she heartily concurs in their belief that, had the Prince Consort been spared, he would have witnessed with intense interest the development of his ideas.

In conclusion Her Majesty says;—

"I cordially agree with you in the prayer that this undertaking may be the means of imparting a stimulus to the commercial interests and intercourse of all parts of my dominions, by encouraging the arts of peace and industry, and by strengthening the bonds of union which now exist in every portion of my empire."

Three hearty cheers are, hereupon, given, the Lord Chamberlain, pronounces the Exhibition open, prayer is offered by the Archbishop of Canterbury; and the "Hallelujah Chorus," and "Home Sweet Home," are sung, after which, and whilst the choir is giving "Rule Britannia," Her Majesty leaves the building, and enters her carriage, amidst the cheers of the multitude outside.

And, here, too, we must close this little record, which Her Majesty has so graciously permitted us to issue, of some of the glad and sorrowful, memorable and deeply interesting scenes in the life of that Royal Family which is so deservedly dear to every loyal-hearted Englishman and woman.

WINDSOR CASTLE.

W. NICHOLSON AND SONS, PRINTERS, WAKEFIELD.

www.ingramcontent.com/pod-product-compliance
Lightning Source LLC
Chambersburg PA
CBHW032140230426
43672CB00011B/2406